Beating Bureaucracy in Special Needs

Are you overwhelmed by the amount of paperwork that SEN generates in your school? Would you like to spend more time actually improving the quality of teaching and learning for pupils with SEN or disabilities? If so, this is an essential book for you.

Containing practical strategies for reducing the number of individual education plans and review meetings, *Beating Bureaucracy in Special Educational Needs* will help you to use existing systems for target setting, recording and planning – personalised systems that are used for all children as part of everyday teaching practices. The book showcases the work of four schools that have successfully developed ways of planning provision, working with parents, and supporting staff development. Ready-to-use proforma in the book are also available online, and include:

- a model policy to give to Ofsted to explain why the school does not use IEPs
- an information sheet for parents
- curriculum planning formats
- strategy sheets that can be highlighted and given to class and subject teachers
- proformas for commonly used interventions that describe the intervention, its target group, its entry and exit criteria, and monitoring and evaluation arrangements.

This invaluable resource will help you (in the words of one SENCO) 'get your life back'. Adopting the new and more effective ways of working presented here will reduce the bureaucratic burden on your school – whilst at the same time improving the impact of your SEN provision on children's learning and well-being.

Jean Gross is a psychologist, writer and lecturer. She has written widely on special needs issues, and until recently led the Primary National Strategy's work on inclusion.

nasen
Helping Everyone Achieve

Other titles published in association with the National Association for Special Educational Needs (nasen):

Teaching Foundation Mathematics: A Guide for Teachers of Older Students with Learning Disabilities
Nadia Naggar-Smith
978-0-415-45164-2

Language for Learning: A Practical Guide for Supporting Pupils with Language and Communication Difficulties across the Curriculum
Sue Hayden
978-1-84312-468-9

The Rob Long Omnibus Edition of Better Behaviour
Rob Long
978-1-84312-470-2

The Special School's Handbook
Michael Farrell
978-0-415-41685-6 (HB)
978-0-415-41686-3 (PB)

The SEN Handbook for Trainee Teachers, NQTs and Teaching Assistants
Wendy Spooner
978-1-84312-404-7

The New nasen A–Z of Reading Resources
Suzanne Baker & Lorraine Petersen
978-1-84312-441-2

P Levels in Mainstream Settings: Meeting the Needs of all Pupils
Lorraine Petersen & Ann Fergusson
(Forthcoming)
978-0-415-43791-2

Diversity and Personalised Learning
John Visser
(Forthcoming)
978-0-415-46752-0

Beating Bureaucracy in Special Educational Needs

Jean Gross

Routledge
Taylor & Francis Group

LONDON AND NEW YORK

nasen
Helping Everyone Achieve

First published 2008
by Routledge
2 Park Square, Milton Park, Abingdon, Oxon OX14 4RN

Simultaneously published in the USA and Canada
by Routledge
270 Madison Ave, New York, NY 10016

Routledge is an imprint of the Taylor & Francis Group, an informa business

This book is published in association with the National Association for
Special Educational Needs (NASEN)

NASEN is a registered charity no. 1007023

© 2008 Jean Gross

Typeset in Garamond by Wearset Ltd, Boldon, Tyne and Wear
Printed and bound in Great Britain by Bell & Bain Ltd, Glasgow

British Library Cataloguing in Publication Data
A catalogue record for this book is available from the British Library

Library of Congress Cataloging in Publication Data
Gross, Jean.
Beating bureaucracy in special educational needs/Jean Gross.
p. cm.
Includes bibliographical references and index.
ISBN 978-00415-44114-8 (pbk. : alk. paper) –
ISBN 978-0-203-92887-5 (ebook) 1. Special education—Great Britain.
2. Special education teachers—Job stress—Great Britain.
3. Classroom management—Great Britain. I. Title.
LC3986.G7G757 2008
371.90943–dc22
2007039719

ISBN10: 0-415-44114-5 (pbk)
ISBN10: 0203-92887-3 (ebk)

ISBN13: 978-0-415-44114-8 (pbk)
ISBN13: 978-0-203-92887-5 (ebk)

nasen is a professional membership association which supports all those who work with or care for children and young people with special and additional educational needs. Members include teachers, teaching assistants, support workers, other educationalists, students and parents.

nasen supports its members through policy documents, journals, its magazine *Special!*, publications, professional development courses, regional networks and newsletters. Its website contains more current information such as responses to government consultations. **nasen's** published documents are held in very high regard both in the UK and internationally.

For all the dedicated SENCOs who have tried so hard, over the past 20 years, to make the unworkable work

Contents

Acknowledgements

I am grateful to staff at Ellingham Primary School, Tolworth Infant and Nursery School, the former Coombe Boys' School, Hall Mead Secondary School, Old Ford Primary and Lyons Park Infant School for their help in providing case study material. Also to Sheffield local authority for permission to use their intervention planning outlines and data collection sheet, to Amanda Corcoran for her ideas on monitoring the quality of interventions, and to Alex Devlin for his idea of using a class handover profile.

A note on terminology

This book is about finding ways to reduce the bureaucracy associated with meeting the needs of children who require something that is 'additional to and different from' what is available to all children, if they are to learn and thrive. Most of this bureaucracy is linked to a statutory framework and associated Code of Practice guidance that uses the term 'SEN' (special educational needs). For this reason the term SEN and/or disability is used in the book, rather than the 'learning difficulties and disabilities' terminology that Ofsted (Office for Standards in Education) uses as a common language across education, health and social services.

The SEN Paperchase

A special education needs coordinator (SENCO) in one large city secondary school recently estimated that her department circulated over 6,000 individual education plan (IEP) sheets every term – one in each subject for 400 pupils, 20 per cent of the school's roll.

This is an extreme example, but it reflects a problem that every teacher who picks up this book will recognise. The problem is the oppressive weight of administration and paperwork generated by the well-intentioned aim that every child with special educational needs will have an individual plan describing their needs, and how the needs will be met.

The volume of paper is not the only problem. Each individual plan generates its own cycle of review dates, discussions and meetings. Once SENCOs or inclusion coordinators (INCOs) have written IEPs or cajoled others into writing them, diary and meeting management becomes a major burden.

As most SENCOs have relatively little non-contact time (one to five hours a week for the majority, according to a 2004 National Union of Teachers survey), this means that they are carrying a heavy workload and are often unable to maintain any sort of work–life balance. It also means that they have little if any time to do the job they would like to be doing – helping teachers plan their lessons with the demands of children with SEN in mind, supporting the work that teaching assistants (TAs) do with individuals and groups, evaluating practice so as to improve the provision made for children, or teaching children directly.

A number of researchers have noted that SENCOs feel swamped by the bureaucracy of their task (Wedell, 2002; Lingard, 2001; Cole, 2005). Lingard, for example, surveyed secondary schools and describes responses such as: 'If I update IEPs three times a year, which my school expects, allowing 15 minutes per pupil, and hold one half hour review meeting a year for every pupil, it will involve me in 275 hours' work per annum.' Wedell analysed messages on the SENCO-forum website and noted that

> SENCOs spend an inordinate proportion of their time keeping up with administration … parents should be regularly consulted about IEPs and there is no way this can be achieved with large numbers of pupils…. Subject teachers are faced with so many individual targets that it becomes impossible to keep track of them.
>
> (Wedell, 2002)

The problems of excessive bureaucracy are not confined to SENCOs. The percentage of children identified nationally as having SEN continues to rise. Between 2005 and 2007, it went up from 17.8 per cent to 19.2 per cent – nearly 90,000 more children were identified as having SEN, even though school rolls fell nationally (DCSF, 2007b). Overall, one in five of all mainstream-school primary schoolchildren are identified, and one in six secondary pupils. This means that on average a teacher in Year 5 (the peak year for SEN numbers) will, in a class of 33, be operating IEPs for around eight children. In schools serving areas of high social deprivation, the numbers will be very much higher, sometimes as many as half the class. Each child will have around four targets on their IEP. That makes at least 32 different targets that the teacher is meant to remember. This is clearly an impossibility.

And if the teacher cannot remember what the targets are, how can they possibly use them in any meaningful way to guide their teaching or the child's learning? This is the real emperor's new clothes of the SEN Code of Practice: the fact, rarely commented on, that teachers (like all human beings) have a useful working memory span of no more than seven to eight items, and that if this is exceeded by over-use of IEPs, those IEPs are likely to become static documents with little impact on progress.

Some schools, however, have found a way out of this maze of paperwork. They have found different, less bureaucratic ways of meeting pupils' SEN – for example by provision mapping, and helping class and subject teachers to record what they will do to support pupils with SEN via their normal curriculum planning.

This book is about sharing these schools' practice. It represents an attempt to liberate SENCOs and INCOs from an excessive workload, whilst at the same time protecting the rights of children, and their parents and carers, to the best possible inclusive teaching and learning.

Why all this paperwork?

The rewards for schools for producing a high volume of paperwork around SEN have until fairly recently been many, enough to outweigh the negative impact on work–life balance and quality of provision. The more children the school logs as having SEN, the more favourably its position in league tables may be judged, if it appears to be under-achieving in its end of key stage SAT (standard assessment test) or GCSE outcomes. The inclusion of numbers of children with SEN in the model that generates contextual value-added (CVA) pupil progress data has compounded this problem; if a school identifies large numbers of children as having SEN, the pupil progress levels predicted by the model will be lower, and the CVA score consequently more favourable.

The IEP, visible indicator of what teachers do to meet SEN, easy to get hold of (in both literal and metaphorical senses) by Ofsted inspectors whose expertise in SEN might be limited, also received heavy emphasis in inspections:

> Some schools had found that inspectors were more interested in the listing, production and number of IEPs than how they related to pupils' achievements and progress … some schools were mechanically producing IEPs for the purposes of inspection, with no planned reviews and no mechanism for their subsequent maintenance.

(Ofsted, 1999)

Until recently, too, funding mechanisms have encouraged schools to focus on paperwork. The more and smarter the IEPs compiled by a school, the more additional local authority (LA) funding attracted through audits or Statements. And, once attracted, the only way to keep funding allocated to individuals was to prove, through voluminous records, that the child was still struggling despite being well supported.

The rewards for plentiful, elegantly executed IEPs were thus once great; the SENCO's credibility, and often his or her 'earning power' for the school, could stand or fall on IEP performance.

But things are changing. Now, an increasing number of local authorities are complying with the plans set out in the government's *Removing barriers to achievement* (DfES, 2004d) and delegating funding for all but the less common (low-incidence) types of SEN to schools. Where this has been done, using a formula based on social deprivation or prior attainment, schools no longer have to submit detailed plans and records for individual children with the more common types of SEN, in order to secure or retain funding.

Ofsted, moreover, is more likely these days to be interested in schools' data on the progress of children with SEN or disabilities, and schools' self-evaluation of the impact of their provision on vulnerable groups, than it is in IEPs.

Another significant development has been the government's policy of 'personalisation'. Personalisation requires schools to assess and plan for the unique needs of every child, not just those identified with SEN or a disability. Together with Assessment for Learning, personalisation has meant that class and subject teachers are increasingly setting personal targets for groups of children, and sometimes for individuals, and involving children in reviewing how far they have achieved them. This increasingly makes redundant the setting and reviewing of individual targets for some children via IEPs.

A final innovation has been provision mapping. First developed by my colleague Ann Berger in Bristol schools, and later incorporated into materials I wrote for the National Strategies, it affords a simple way of recording the extra interventions that the school provides in each year group. A teacher or SENCO/INCO can highlight on the provision map the interventions that a particular child receives, and use this, together with personal targets set by the class or subject teacher, as an alternative to writing separate individual plans.

What is stopping schools from reducing bureaucracy?

Despite the system changes that ought to be helping schools to reduce bureaucracy, there is as yet little evidence of the widespread changes that might be expected.

Seven years ago I wrote an article, 'Paper promises' (Gross, 2000), that described the overwhelming burden of paperwork that schools were experiencing and suggested ways of achieving the ends of the SEN Code of Practice by different means.

But seven years later, I still see many SENCOs/INCOs and teachers struggling to manage large numbers of IEPs, meetings and reviews, now compounded by new requirements, such as school self-evaluation, disability planning, and the expectations in the Every Child Matters framework that they also manage multi-agency working in their settings.

The government's Implementation Review Group, made up of headteachers and union representatives and charged with working with government to reduce bureaucratic burdens on schools, notes that SEN is the area where least progress has been made:

> In all our many and wide-ranging contacts with people in schools we hear time and time again that Special Educational Needs (SEN) is the area where change is most needed.

(IRU, 2006)

The lack of change is in spite of clarifications issued by government making it clear that IEPs are not a statutory requirement.

EXTRACT

From *Effective leadership: ensuring the progress of pupils with SEN and/or disabilities* (DfES, 2006a)

The SEN Code of Practice (2001) reflected common practice in describing individual education plans (IEPs) as one method by which the process of target setting, planning provision and review could be carried out. Many schools and LAs are confused about the status of IEPs and whether or not they are always necessary. IEPs can be an area where there is unnecessary paperwork and duplication.

An IEP is a teaching and planning tool with:

- no more than three or four targets;
- appropriate strategies;
- a record of the outcomes.

IEPs are not a statutory requirement. Where schools have a policy of individual planning and recording for all pupils then the pupil with SEN should not need an IEP. The National Strategies provide examples of how to record interventions as part of class lesson plans with a record of the pupil's progress – the outcomes of the intervention – being recorded in the same way as for all other pupils.

...Where provision mapping is linked to recording outcomes for all pupils or other locally devised systems and personalised learning initiatives are in place, they should gradually replace IEPs for most if not all pupils while still providing the reassurance and accountability to parents/carers that is so important.

EXTRACT

From *Meeting need – minimising bureaucracy* (IRU, 2007)
Schools do not need to write individual education plans for children with SEN where they have a policy of planning, target setting and recording the progress for all pupils as part of personalised learning that:

- Identifies learning targets for individual pupils
- Plans additional or different provision from the differentiated curriculum offered to all pupils
- Reviews provision in the light of individual pupil outcomes.

So what is it that is stopping schools from taking this advice? There seem to be a number of factors:

- Poor communication by local authorities with heads and SENCOs/INCOs, so that many schools fail to understand that they can identify a child as having SEN without necessarily going through a full IEP planning process.
- Local authority encouragement to schools to provide provision maps as well as, rather than instead of, IEPs.
- Pressure from class teachers, who believe that maintaining an IEP for a child will mean that the child gets support, usually in the form of a teaching assistant.
- Concerns about parents' reactions if the IEP process or the linked push for Statements are not used.
- A historical belief that the quality and quantity of paperwork is the key to attracting and retaining funding.
- A belief that IEPs make a difference to pupil outcomes.

Do IEPs make a difference?

All the paperwork involved in SEN would be well worth doing if we knew that it was actually making a real difference to children. But is there any evidence of this?

Schools tend to think there is, because they see children achieving the small-steps targets set for them on IEPs. There is a circularity, however, in school self-evaluation forms and school profiles claiming proudly that children are achieving the targets set on their IEPs, when the targets are required to be set from the start as specific, measurable, **achievable**, realistic and time-constrained. The key factor is whether the achievement of a series of these achievable targets aggregates, over time, into improved attainment, or improved personal and life skills. National data, as we will see later, suggests that the procedures of the SEN Code have not so far led to these improved outcomes.

Schools have historically embarked on the paperwork involved in SEN for one main reason – the quest for additional resources. And yet those resources, once painfully attained, may in fact make little difference to the child's progress. Pinney (2004) analysed a wide range of national statistics and found no link between the numbers of Statements maintained by local authorities and the results achieved by their pupils with SEN. Ofsted's *Annual Report of Her Majesty's Chief Inspector of Schools* (2006b) noted that:

> The SEN Code of Practice has some serious weaknesses in operation. First, the provision of additional resources to pupils – such as teaching assistant support – does not ensure good-quality intervention or adequate pupil progress.

Ofsted found little evidence for the impact of Statements of SEN in the survey that led to the report *Inclusion: does it matter where pupils are taught* (2006a):

> A statement of SEN usually generated additional resources, but even if this guaranteed the quantity of provision, it did nothing to determine the quality of provision or outcomes for pupils in any type of setting … in case studies of pupils with ASD, SLD and pupils with physical disabilities and difficulties, the process of formal assessment had helped to determine the interventions that were required but had no impact on the outcomes for pupils.

And an earlier research report, *Special educational needs and disability: towards inclusive schools* (Ofsted, 2004) concluded that for pupils with SEN or disabilities at any stage of the SEN Code:

> Expectations of pupil achievement are often neither well enough defined, nor pitched high enough. Progress in learning remains slower than it should be for a significant number of pupils.

This is most evident for pupils with literacy and numeracy difficulties – the most common type of SEN. Table 1.1 shows the percentage of children leaving primary school with severe difficulties in these areas (achieving below National Curriculum Level 3 at the end of Key Stage 2).

	1998	1999	2000	2001	2002	2003	2004	2005	2006
ENGLISH	7*	7	6	7	7	6.7	6.9	6.3	6.1
MATHEMATICS	7	6	6	5	5	6.3	6.1	5.8	6.0

TABLE 1.1 Percentage and numbers achieving below Level 3 in English and mathematics

Note: *Pre-2003 data is only available rounded to the nearest percentage.

Since 1998 the percentage of children with very low attainment at the end of primary school has hovered round the 6–7 per cent mark, despite ever-increasing numbers identified as having SEN and placed on the SEN Code procedures, and despite any number of IEPs which continue predominantly to focus on literacy and numeracy as their prime targets. All those targets, written by thousands of schools on millions of IEPs – 'Will learn to read first 50 high-frequency words', 'Will be able to read cvc words', 'Will know number bonds to ten' – appear to have had little impact. All the training provided to teachers on how to write specific, measurable, achievable and time-constrained (SMART) targets, how to select appropriate strategies to achieve them, and how to measure and document the outcomes, appears to have made no difference at all to the numbers of children failing to learn to read or understand and use the number system.

Where there have begun to be signs of a downward trend in the numbers experiencing significant difficulties, as in English between 2004 and 2006, this has not been the result of more individual planning for children, but instead has coincided with a national focus on improving the actual **provision** made in schools. It has coincided with the training provided to schools on choosing and implementing effective, evidence-based Wave 3 literacy intervention programmes for individuals and groups. The evidence suggests that it is provision, not paperwork, that makes the difference to children's attainment.

A similarly static national picture applies to pupils with significant literacy and numeracy difficulties in secondary schools. In KS3, currently only around 50 per cent of pupils who have SEN and who attained a Level 4 in science, mathematics or English at the end of KS2 go on to achieve Level 5 by the end of KS3.

Nor do the procedures of the SEN Code appear to have had much effect on reducing the frequency of behaviour difficulties. Exclusions have not gone down over the period when more and more children were placed on individual education or behaviour plans because of behavioural, emotional or social difficulties. Being identified as having SEN does not appear to afford particular protection to such pupils; the Audit Commission (2002) found that pupils so identified made up 87 per cent of exclusions in primary schools and 60 per cent of exclusions in secondary schools.

The only area where it is possible that the SEN Code's procedures have made a difference may be personal and life skills, but here we have no evidence at all either way, since we have as yet no agreed means of assessing and recording children's development in these areas, nor definitions of what would constitute an average, above-average or below-average rate of progress.

In sum, the evidence that all the work schools have put into implementing the SEN Code procedures is justified by the impact is slender, to say the least. And in schools where it has proved possible to bring about significant reductions in the numbers of children failing to achieve basic literacy, numeracy or social, emotional and behavioural skills, this has not been through having more children on the SEN register, or more and better IEPs. Instead, these gains have been produced by changing the way groups and classes of children have been taught, using the kinds of inclusive classroom teaching strategies and evidence-based additional interventions described later on in this book, in Chapters 6 and 7.

The problem with the individual model

The Code of Practice rests on the identification of individual children's difficulties, and the targeting of resources to address their perceived problems. Many writers have commented on the inadequacies of this individual model. Their argument has been that it shifts responsibility away from what schools as institutions might do to better meet the needs of all learners, towards a model which seeks to prop up the child identified as different (and by implication deficient) in accessing an otherwise undifferentiated curriculum through the provision of additional individual adult support.

An example comes from the illuminating story told by David Moore, Her Majesty's Inspector, who observed a secondary class being taught about the workings of the spinning jenny. The worksheets used were difficult, and the TA who was supporting one young man (herself with a physics degree) had to go and ask the teacher what they meant. 'Don't get worried', the boy said to her, 'I never do.' When HMI asked him why he never got worried, he replied 'Cos she's always here to do the work for me, in't she?'

A model based on the identification of individual children's difficulties thus often prevents teachers from differentiating the curriculum. It may also serve to lower expectations for what children with SEN or disabilities can achieve. A recent piece of research (Tymms and Merrell, 2006) compared the progress of children who had been formally identified through screening procedures as having SEN (in this case, attention deficit hyperactivity disorder (ADHD)) with those who also had ADHD symptoms but where the child's class teacher was not told of this, nor SEN procedures invoked. The teachers of this second group were simply given general information about how to teach inattentive and hyperactive children. The teachers in the first group were provided with both this information and the names of children identified through screening.

Providing information on teaching strategies was helpful; children in the second group had more positive attitudes towards school and reading, and showed improved behaviour, when compared with children in schools not given the teaching information. But formally identifying children as having ADHD was not helpful; the researchers found a significant negative effect on the reading and mathematics attainment of children who had been identified as having ADHD, when compared with children not identified. They suggest that this is because, once labelled, teachers focus more on keeping the children happy and calm rather than pushing them to attain. Equally, it might mean that teachers relinquished more of the care of the children to additional adults, rather than working with them directly themselves.

What this research and anecdote suggests is that over-reliance on identifying SEN and invoking the associated procedures can sometimes mean that the teacher who is responsible for the child's learning may do less to adapt his or her curriculum delivery than if the child were not identified. This is a direct consequence of the individual model of SEN, and of the way in which IEP targets for change are located with the child and not with the teacher.

The problem with IEP targets

To understand the problem with IEP targets we need to understand who they belong to. Targets **do** work: we have only to look at the increase in the number of children achieving Level 4s at the end of KS2, Level 5s at the end of KS3, and 5 good GCSEs, to see this. Most education professionals have by now experienced for themselves the powerful effects of working towards a target for which they felt personally accountable, and which was clear, measurable and time-constrained.

The targets we have all as individuals experienced, however, have one thing in common: for them to work, we needed to know what they were, and to be constantly reminded of them, frequently monitored on them, and recognised if we achieved them. Yet if we undertake the exercise of asking children with SEN what their IEP targets are, we consistently find that they have no idea: 'the views of the pupils are rarely sought in the preparation of IEPs or in the review process' (Ofsted, 1999). The targets may have been made up by the SENCO sitting at home with her paperwork, or they may have been spawned by a computer programme. Even if the child was involved originally in agreeing targets, the chances are that no one has reminded him or her of them since then.

There are other problems with targets as well as the problem of confused ownership. Individual-child targets also have a habit of replacing meaningful hopes and dreams with what can be readily measured. The drive to get SMART has meant, at worst, a generation of children (and of the adults round them) who believe that staying in their seat for five minutes, not tearing up their work, or packing their bag before school in the morning, will magically make them be able to concentrate, to believe in themselves, or be well organised. We tend to forget that teachers and children still need this broader sense of where they meaningfully want to get to in the end, as well as the tiny, achievable, tickable targets along the way. Reaching these targets may well mean that deeper objectives are beginning to be achieved, may act as 'success criteria' for the achievement of the objectives, but they cannot and should not substitute for them.

Effective interventions for children with SEN or disabilities, moreover, are often far too complex to reduce to a few SMART targets. The highly effective Reading Recovery literacy intervention provides half an hour of daily one-to-one teaching for a period of 12 to 20 weeks. Each day, the highly trained Reading Recovery teacher assesses the child's knowledge and skills. Each day, they plan what they will teach on the basis of this assessment. The teaching on any one day might include a new grapheme–phoneme link; a way of breaking a word into chunks, how to use phrasing and expression when reading aloud, a way of forming a letter, how to hold a sentence of increasing length in the mind while writing it, how to write an irregular but common word quickly and fluently. How could all this be expressed in a small number of termly SMART targets?

Consider another effective intervention, this time for children with social, emotional and behaviour difficulties – placement in a nurture group. Such a placement involves around two terms in a small group of around 12 children, working all day every day in a family-like environment to learn the basics of how to relate to others, to share, to concentrate, to listen, to talk. Again, how can all this essential and ever-changing learning be described in a limited number of targets?

And what would be added to either the nurture group provision, or the Reading Recovery teaching, by writing an IEP for the children taking part? In both cases, we have a skilled teacher who is constantly developing, monitoring and reviewing targets for what they want the child to achieve. In both cases, they may well articulate for the child what it is that the child needs to focus on – 'Today, I want to see you…', 'What I'm looking for when you read this book is that you…'. But they will not waste precious teaching time on writing half-termly or termly paper plans for every child they work with.

The importance of talking

IEPs were never intended to be just bits of paper, recording measurable but over-simple and often meaningless targets in the absence of ownership or involvement of the person potentially most willing and able to put in the energy needed to achieve them – the child him- or herself.

Before the paperchase began in earnest, when there were fewer IEPs and those there were had a less bureaucratic purpose, the IEP was just the written record of a much more important human process. This process was about **talking**. It brought together all the people most concerned about the child's progress (parent/carer, teacher and child) at a meeting whose purpose was to share information, clarify the broad objectives for the child's progress, remind everyone of the child's strengths, and arrive collaboratively at some priority targets to which all present could subscribe and all contribute.

Properly done, this kind of meeting – including deciding who will do what to help the child reach the priority targets – takes about an hour. To be effective, it needs to be followed by frequent monitoring of the agreed actions, and frequent monitoring of progress, in a way which keeps the targets alive for the child. There must be a review date set not so far away that participants can forget that they will at that date be held to account for the success or failure of the joint enterprise – more than a term will be too long, and less would be better.

From this it is clear that in all but the most favoured schools, usually small primaries with no more than one or two pupils per class with identified SEN, it will not be possible to implement the talking model of IEP planning successfully. No teacher with more children than this number on the register will be willing to hold that many meetings or reviews. We know that the majority of schools do not: one Ofsted (1999) survey found that most schools reviewed their IEPs formally (i.e. at a meeting involving parents) only once a year.

This is why a potentially energising, effective means of joint planning, admirable in its intent, has degenerated into a paper exercise. In these circumstances, it is important to consider whether it is worth doing at all, or whether there might not be other, better ways of planning which will maximise the achievement of pupils with SEN.

Schools may decide that they need to focus the full, teacher-dependent planning process on only those children who need a fresh, concerted, home–school impetus to move them on, and those with the most complex needs. These schools will adopt simpler systems for meeting additional needs – for the broad range of children with learning or emotional and behavioural difficulties.

In doing so, they will go back to first principles and consider what essential functions the SEN bureaucracy was meant to achieve, so as to decide how those functions might be met in different and less paper-driven ways. In this book, we will take each of these functions in turn, and describe ways of fulfilling them that are manageable, effective and non-bureaucratic.

But first, let us look at some case studies of schools that have made progress in reducing bureaucracy, at the systems they have introduced, and at the impact.

2 | Case Studies

1: Ellingham Primary School

Ellingham school is a one-form entry primary with 238 pupils on roll. It serves an area of mixed housing, some of which is local authority and some owner-occupied. The number of English as an additional language (EAL) learners is growing and minority ethnic groups now make up 20 per cent of the children on roll. A total of 12 per cent of pupils have been identified as having SEN.

The inclusion coordinator is also the deputy head. When she took on the responsibility for inclusion three years ago, she asked staff what they did with IEPs once they were written. Usually, staff said they just put them in a drawer. When asked whether they looked at them between reviews, they said that they generally didn't. She then investigated whether IEPs were helping to secure parental involvement and found that parents were invited in to sign the IEP or review, but were generally not doing anything to help the children achieve their targets. In discussion with the borough's SEN adviser, she decided to replace IEPs with a new system for setting targets, monitoring progress and involving families.

The system revolves around five key processes:

1 personal target-setting and review through 'Learning Logs';
2 communicating children's needs through 'Communication Passports';
3 curriculum planning for differentiation;
4 the involvement of parents and carers in their child's learning;
5 provision mapping.

Personal target setting and review through 'Learning Logs'

The school was already in the process of developing a system through which all children would set personal targets for their learning and development. The INCO stresses that reducing SEN bureaucracy would not have been possible without this. The focus is on children owning their own learning – setting targets (with their teacher's help), deciding on what evidence will show that they have met them, gathering the evidence, and discussing the evidence with the teacher. This face-to-face discussion has in many cases eliminated the need for teachers to spend hours marking children's work when the child is not present.

Every child keeps a record of their personal targets, one in each of the core subjects plus one in another area such as personal development or behaviour. Examples would be 'To get better at roly-polys without balancing on my head', 'To tell back a story', 'To learn my 2 x tables'. Children in the Foundation Stage and Key Stage 1 set one or two targets per half term. Year 3 and 4 children set between one and three a week, and Year 5 and 6 set one to three targets daily or weekly as appropriate.

All the children, including those with SEN, are very clear what their targets are. Time is allocated on Mondays and Fridays to setting targets and reviewing progress towards them. Children record their self-assessments in a 'Learning Log' (a single book containing all their final pieces of work in all subjects). An example is shown in Figure 2.1.

The school uses Essex Target Tracker (www.targettrackersolutions.org) to track children's overall progress and help children identify what they need to learn next. Numerical targets (National Curriculum levels and sub-levels, including 'P' levels) are broken down to show evidence of achievement at each sub-level. Children use these evidence statements to help them set

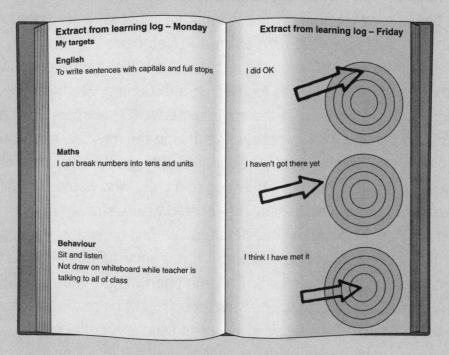

FIGURE 2.1 Extracts from learning log

their own targets and to self-assess. They might, for example, highlight a section in a piece of work in their Learning Log and note that it provides evidence of achievement of a target they have set themselves. Teachers also write notes in the Learning Log to show how and when children have met their learning targets.

Communicating children's needs through 'Communication Passports'

As well as their Learning Log, each child with SEN also has a Communication Passport (Table 2.1). These laminated sheets describe the child's strengths, interests, areas of difficulty and the strategies that help them. They are framed in the child's own language, and serve to make sure that everyone who works with the child is familiar with their profile and can access it to plan for teaching and learning.

Staff meetings have a slot called 'Children update', where everyone is briefed on issues affecting individual children and on areas they are working on ('This week X is trying to ... please try to notice when he manages it'). The same information is shared at lunchtime supervisors' meetings, so that they also form part of the supportive team around the child.

Curriculum planning

Teaching and learning for the child with SEN is shaped through teachers' regular curriculum planning, rather than separate paperwork. Half-termly plans (Table 2.2) have additional columns for staff to note the strategies that will be deployed to support the learning of those who are gifted and talented, have SEN or a disability, or are EAL learners.

Regular training for staff helps them to develop skills in differentiation. Recent training, for example, has focused on questioning. Staff learned how to use higher-order questions for gifted and talented (G&T) learners. For children with learning difficulties they practised identifying the most basic question to ask in a hierarchical sequence of question difficulty, and asking other children similar questions before putting a question to a child who would benefit from the models provided by classmates. They shared useful strategies for questioning, such as posing the question then pairing a child with a chat buddy to talk to before answering, and adopting TV quiz show ideas ('Phone a friend', 'Take someone with you' and so on). Children often work in mixed ability collaborative groups where any one of the group might be asked to answer a question, and rewards (tokens) are given for the success of the group as a whole. This means the group has to make sure that all its members, including those with SEN, understand the topic and are able to answer questions.

Involvement of parents and carers in their child's learning

Parental involvement is fundamental to the work of the school. The local authority Social Inclusion Service has been brought in to run parenting workshops, covering issues such as behaviour, family relationships, self-esteem and relaxation. The INCO has been much involved in development work in the local cluster of schools, which now run shared workshops for parents, such as the Family Learning 'Keeping up with the children' course. All parents are invited to these courses, but those whose children have difficulties in literacy or mathematics are particularly encouraged to attend. Focus groups of parents in the cluster were surveyed to find out what kinds of support they wanted, and what would make it easier for them to take part in school events. This led to the provision of crèche facilities run by trusted adults from the school, and meetings for parents learning EAL that were held in the nursery so that their children could play at their feet. Invitations to join events and courses are on brightly coloured slips of paper; refreshments are provided; and certificates used to reward attendance.

The INCO inherited a number of letters and proformas for communication with parents/carers of children with SEN, but has found it more helpful to do everything by personal contact, either face to face or on the telephone.

SEN reviews are held twice a year but incorporated within regular parents' evenings. Where children have SEN, the parents' evening meeting is scheduled to take half an hour rather than ten minutes. The INCO attends these meetings and takes brief notes there and then on a simple review sheet (Table 2.3).

Before the parents' evening, cover is arranged to allow every class teacher to meet the INCO and do a 'class review'. They will discuss every child with additional needs (SEN or disability, gifted and talented, EAL). The review takes about an hour per class and is typed up during the meeting. The meeting generates referral lists for outside agencies, including the names of children who would benefit from structured buddy support or who can lend such support to younger children. It also forms the basis of the audit of needs that shapes the school's provision map.

Provision mapping

Additional provision for individuals and groups is planned annually with adjustments made mid-year. The provision map is planned by SEN need type and includes:

For communication and interaction: social skills rehearsal groups, social stories, in-class support using visual calendars and timetables, individual speech and language programmes devised by a speech and language therapist.

For cognition and learning: phonics groups, Numbershark with a buddy, '15 minutes a day' literacy programme, reading with an older buddy, memory work with a buddy.

For behavioural, social and emotional needs: nurture/breakfast clubs, daily 'nurture chats' with TA and INCO.

For sensory and physical needs: a fine motor skills intervention called Jump Ahead, individual speech and language programmes devised by an occupational therapist.

Peer support is extensively employed, as well as adult support. The INCO has trained peer buddies to work with a partner on reading, ICT and memory skills.

The provision afforded to each child is shown on the overall map and can be used if necessary, together with the Communication Passport, extracts from the Learning Log, examples of teachers' differentiated planning and notes from class reviews and parents' evenings, to supply evidence of what the school has done to meet the child's needs.

Other ways of beating bureaucracy

The INCO's other tips for reducing bureaucracy include making good use of the internet and work in local clusters or networks of schools. Via the internet, for example, she located audit tools (from the CSIE Index for Inclusion and Birmingham's Inclusion Standard) to help her develop her school's accessibility plan. The net also proved valuable in developing school policies, as did examples from other schools in her local cluster. This local extended schools/ECM cluster has proved an excellent source of ideas; the schools in the cluster submit shared bids for funding and through this have managed to employ a shared family liaison worker, run social skills groups, and offer shared SEN training to support staff.

Communication Passport

| Child's photograph | **NAME:** A
D.O.B.
SEN Stage: School Action Plus
SEN Support Began: Spring 2002
Areas of Concern: Cognition and learning, social, emotional and behavioural skills |

WHAT DO I FIND EASY?

Drawing and painting

Tracing

WHAT DO I LIKE DOING?

Drawing and colouring

Drama

Making up stories

Art club – 'but it's not for very long, you could bring something to eat and we could stay later!'

PE, especially gym

Getting stuff from magazines and making collages

WHAT CAN I DO INDEPENDENTLY?

All art especially drawing and colouring

Sequencing a picture story

Ideas for stories

Some spellings

Setting up games

Making up my own games 'but Morgan doesn't usually want to play'

WHAT DO I FIND HARD?

All maths

Some science

Trying to study when other people are talking

Writing quickly

WHAT DON'T I LIKE DOING?

Everything, except art

'I hate maths.'

Setting my own targets from the board

Sitting with boys

Filing work in folders — 'I just sling it in my desk!'

WHAT DO I NEED SUPPORT WITH?

Maths – 'I like maths games but not all that adding up and stuff.'

Writing – 'Don't give me so much because I get worn out, I would like somebody to write for me.' 'I would like a square pen because I keep forgetting to hold it right and I'm worried about losing my handwriting licence.'

'If a teacher sat on the carpet they could help other people and me.'

Communication Passport – reverse side	
Support received	
Year 2	Small group work with support of TA
	Extra reading sessions 2 to 3 × weekly with TA and parent helpers
	Phonological Awareness Training (PAT) (1 term)
Year 3	Small group work with support of TA
	Increased computer access for writing
	Jump Ahead – 3 × weekly
	OT box of activities
	Extra reading sessions 2 to 3 × weekly with TA and parent helpers A peer reading partner to share school reading book
	TA to scribe R's ideas if it involves lots of writing
	Interactive ICT maths games: Numbershark
	Increasing involvement of EP
Year 4	Small group work with support of TA – breaking tasks and concepts down into manageable chunks for R to understand
	Jump Ahead fine motor skills 5 × weekly
	OT box of activities 5 × weekly
	Reading sessions with TA and a parent helper 2 × weekly
	Interactive ICT maths games: Numbershark 3 × weekly
	Social Inclusion Support Service involved (HW)
	Involvement of EP
Year 5	
Year 6	

TABLE 2.1 A Communication Passport

HALF-TERMLY YEAR 2 LITERACY PLANNING

	KEY QUESTIONS AND ACTIVITIES	ICT/RESOURCES/SUPPORT	LEARNING INTENTIONS
WEEK 1	**Can you retell the story of *The Very Hungry Caterpillar?*** As a class read and discuss the story. Children to rewrite the story but using different food. (Focus beginning, middle and end and paragraphs). Children to use dictionary to find different foods. **LINK ICT – (See ICT planning).** **Can you rewrite sentences in correct order adding punctuation?** Work to be done in ICT suite. **Guided reading – numbers – link with maths. Spelling – daily – PAT? Handwriting – lower case c, a, o, e.**	*The Very Hungry Caterpillar* Dictionary Learning mats Word books LCP card – Numbers (1)	To be aware of the difference between spoken and written language.
G&T & HOTS (Analysis, Synthesis, Evaluation)	<u>Child A and Child B</u> Synthesis – Can you write your own story using a different character and different food?		
SEN	<u>Child C and Child D</u> Writing 3 key sentences from VHC using story frame and word book.		
EAL	<u>Child E, F and G</u> Vocab: caterpillar, cocoon and butterfly and food names.		
WEEK 2	**What happened before and after this picture?** Children given a middle action picture from baby catalogue book. Children use planning sheet to show what happened before and after the picture. From planning sheets children write the story (focus beginning, middle and end) 3 paragraphs. **LINK ICT – (See ICT planning).**	The baby catalogue Planning sheets Order	To understand about beginnings, middles and ends. To understand time and sequential events in stories i.e. what happened when?

TABLE 2.2 An example of a half-termly plan

	Content	Resources	Objectives
	Can you rewrite sentences in the correct order adding punctuation? **Work to be done in ICT suite.** **Guided reading – joining in – link PSHE.** **Spelling – daily – PAT?** **Handwriting – r, n, m, u.**	LCP card – Joining In (16)	To check work through and add adjectives where appropriate.
G&T & HOTS (Analysis, Synthesis, Evaluation)	<u>Child A and Child B</u> Analysis – which words could you add to make your story more interesting?		
SEN	<u>Child C and Child D</u> Sequence pictures in order and oral retelling.		
EAL	<u>Child E, F and G</u> Tell and plan story first in home language. Vocabulary beginning, middle, end.		
WEEK 3	**LINK – ART** **Why did the bears chase Goldilocks?** Children to write about favourite event in Goldilocks. Drama – children to work in small groups to act out the story. Hot-seating characters. Children to rewrite the story with clear beginning, middle and end – focus on adjectives. **LINK ICT – (See ICT planning).** **Can you put words from a word bank into your own sentences?** Work to be done in ICT suite. **Guided reading – 2D or 3D – link maths.** **Spelling – daily – PAT?** **Handwriting – v, w, x.**	*Goldilocks and the Three Bears* LCP 2,1,3,4 Word books Dictionaries Learning mats LCP card – 2D or 3D (32)	To identify and discuss reasons for events in stories, linked to the plot.

TABLE 2.2 continued

G&T & HOTS (Analysis, Synthesis, Evaluation)	<u>Child A and Child B</u> Evaluation – How would you structure 5 clear paragraphs for *Goldilocks and the Three Bears*?		
SEN	<u>Child C and Child D</u> Use Clicker software to write a sentence for the beginning, middle and end of the story.		
EAL	<u>Child E, F and G</u> Work with TA to act out story with puppets before rewriting.		
WEEK 4	**What happened after Rosie left her hutch?** Read – retell the story of Rosie's walk. Drama – act out the story with children pretending to be different characters. Rewrite the story using own linking words. Going on a word hunt (LCP 2144) – writing sentences using these linking words. **LINK ICT – (See ICT planning).** **Can you replace 'and' and 'then' with better linking words?** Work to be done in ICT suite. **Spelling – daily – PAT?** **Handwriting – l, t, h, b, k.**	*Rosie's Walk* List of linking words (after, meanwhile, then, next and after a while) Going on a word hunt LCP 2,1,4,4 Word books Dictionaries Learning Mats	To use the language to structure a sequence of events.
G&T & HOTS (Analysis, Synthesis, Evaluation)	<u>Child A and Child B</u> Synthesis – Can you rewrite the story as if you were the fox?		
SEN	<u>Child C and Child D</u> Insert linking words into a teacher-provided story	Teacher-provided story.	

TABLE **2.2** continued

23

				To understand about beginnings, middles and ends. To understand time and sequential events in stories i.e. what happened when?
EAL	Child E, F and G Vocab: then, next, after, before, meanwhile.			
WEEK 5	**ASSESSMENT WEEK** **What happened before and after this picture?** Children given a different middle action picture taken from baby catalogue book. Children use planning sheet to show what happened before and after the picture. From planning sheets children write the story (focus beginning, middle and end) 3 paragraphs. **LINK ICT – (See ICT planning).** **Can you replace 'and' and 'then' with better linking words?** Work to be done in ICT suite. Spelling – daily – PAT? Handwriting – j, y, g, p, q. **Guided reading – Help! Dial 999 – Link PSHE, history and science.**	Baby catalogue Planning sheets LCP card – Help! dial 999 (30)		
G&T & HOTS (Analysis, Synthesis, Evaluation)	As assessment – by outcome			
SEN	To retell their story to an adult before writing it.			
EAL	To retell their story to an adult before writing it.			

TABLE 2.2 continued

SEN Review Summer 2005

Issues discussed, including overview of input this year, successes, areas for development and future targets

School needs to monitor occupational therapy position with view to getting X reinstated.

Finds maths really hard but has made progress in her writing – ideas are good, needs help with recording.

Has recently had a 'blip' with behaviour – hasn't enjoyed being out of routine, has 'wandered' out of lessons.

School to involve Dad in appointments – after school, evening.

Needs lots of practice in holding a pencil.

Continue with Numbershark, next stage of Jump Ahead.

Continue to work in small group.

Parent comments

X discharged because Mrs H (OT) is leaving!
Pleased with reading progress.
Still concerned about comments from A – continue to monitor next year.
Has tantrums/indecisiveness at home.
X to continue Mrs D's club.

Statutory Assessment was discussed but Ms L does not want X to go forward at this stage. V concerned re. experience of her nephew, placement for X and secondary transition.

Date: 11/07/05   Signed:

SEN Review Spring 2006

X continues to be supported in a small group – increasingly needing 1:1 support.
Jump Ahead fine motor skills programme is working well.
School hopes that X will benefit from inclusion in social communication 'Talkabout' group and that through 1:1 nurture chats with Mrs W, self-esteem will be raised.
X v. keen to be involved in setting up of art club – has already chatted to Mrs C about this.
School continues to be concerned re. X's academic and social progress.
V pleased that parents supportive of statutory assessment request.

Parent comments

Feel that X would benefit from working with Yr 6 'buddy' on computers at lunch break.

Date: 24/01/06   Signed:

TABLE 2.3 SEN review sheets

25

CASE STUDY

2: Tolworth Infant and Nursery School

Tolworth is a three-form entry infant and nursery school with 282 children on roll. It serves an area of great social contrasts. A third of children are EAL learners, most at the early stages of English acquisition. Some 26 different languages are spoken in school. A total of 39 per cent of pupils are eligible for free school meals.

The school has both an inclusion coordinator, Rachel Nye (also assessment coordinator and deputy head), and a SENCO. Rachel brings assessment, maths and EAL expertise to her role; the SENCO brings her specialist SEN expertise; the headteacher, Elaine Joyce, a particular understanding of child safeguarding and well-being. Together they form a strong team, which promotes a personalised approach to all children's learning rather than special systems just for those with SEN. The ease with which staff personalise learning springs, Elaine feels, from the early years ethos that now extends right through to Year 2 – an ethos that focuses on where each individual is in their learning ('stage not age', as she describes it), and adapts teaching accordingly.

Inclusive planning and teaching

The school generally only uses IEPs for Statemented children. The strategies adopted to support children with SEN or disabilities are not tucked away in drawers, but visible on the walls. Makaton signs are everywhere. Small posters (Table 2.4) remind staff first of general inclusive teaching strategies, then of strategies for particular children.

To encourage positive behaviour in this class we try to:
- Repeat instructions three times
- Use children's names
- Say 'I feel sad when ...'

Strategies to support TB
- Ignore as much low-level attention seeking as possible
- Attend to him doing the right thing using descriptive praise
- Two areas of focus:
  - doing what an adult says;
  - kind hands and feet (no hurting).
Rewards:

TABLE 2.4 Posters to remind staff of inclusive strategies

A high level of training has gone into developing staff practice in inclusive teaching. Rachel cites in particular the work that has been done on visual supports for learning – highly necessary given the numbers of EAL learners, but hugely beneficial for other children with language difficulties, autism and Down's syndrome. Rachel spends time monitoring the quality of inclusive learning and teaching, and consequent staff development, for example, helping teaching assistants learn to stand back from children they are supporting, so as to foster independence rather than dependence.

All staff make specific notes on their planning to show how they will differentiate learning for higher-, middle- and lower-attaining groups. They then annotate these plans further to show what will be done to support the learning of children who have particular individual needs. Table 2.5 shows an example from the Foundation Stage.

The curriculum is geared to meet the identified needs of the intake – a very high focus on speaking and listening, for example, with lots of drama and role play. There is a policy of reading the children at least three stories a day, carefully chosen to have repetitive language just above the children's own level.

Provision mapping

Although most work to support children with additional needs comes through everyday inclusive teaching for all children, the school also funds a great deal of extra targeted provision for groups and individuals. For example, an additional nursery nurse is employed to focus on early intervention programmes. All staff know that if a child is not making progress then that is not just their concern, but a collective responsibility and an indication that an additional intervention should be put in. Provision (Table 2.6) is made for children experiencing stress or who are anxious and withdrawn (nurturing groups), for social skills development, for motor skills, for oral language skills, literacy and mathematics. All the extra provision is monitored – as Rachel says 'to make sure the children aren't just coming out for nothing'. Expert teacher time (from a specialist maths teacher and a trained former Reading Recovery teacher) is allocated to both working directly with children and to monitoring and supporting the work of the TAs running the intervention programmes.

Tracking progress and setting targets

Despite below-average levels of attainment on entry, children at Tolworth achieve at least as well as the national average at the end of Key Stage 1.

LEARNING AREA	KEY WEEKLY LEARNING OBJECTIVES/ASSESSMENT OPPORTUNITIES HIGHLIGHTED	ADULT-DIRECTED ACTIVITIES	DIFFERENTIATION	SELF-DIRECTED ACTIVITIES AND EXPLORATIONS	EVALUATION/NEXT STEPS
PHSE	To say when something is fair or unfair. To say how it feels when things are unfair.	SEAL relationships lesson – story 'It's not fair'. Make rotas to water plants, look after tadpoles, feed slugs and snails.	H/A – Describe a situation that has not been fair, draw out/discuss when unfairness can be an accident. M/A – Describe a situation that has not been fair. L/A – sort situation photos into fair/unfair and discuss associated feelings – GL – Use feeling dice. EAL – Pre-teach 'It's not fair' story using role play, pics.	Follow rotas for watering plants and looking after tadpoles, etc.	Tadpole diary – whole class majority could say what was fair/unfair – NS and TP need more on this.
Creative	To explore loud and quiet sounds.	Music – express growth and change. The special drum – how does the sound grow?	H/A – Sing and accompany a song which gets louder and quieter. M/A – Respond with body movements to loud and quiet music. L/A – Play drums loudly or softly in response to a graphic symbol.	Use musical instruments in outside area.	
Physical	To use small equipment using basic skills.	Control ball when patting down or up.	H/A, M/A – Pat a ball up and down. L/A – Pat a bean bag in the air. GL – Play with a large ball.	Use tennis bats and bean bags.	

Key: H/A higher attaining, M/A middle attaining, L/A lower attaining. GL is a child with Down's syndrome.

TABLE 2.5 Weekly Foundation Stage planning

	LANGUAGE	LITERACY	MATHS	PHSE	MOTOR SKILLS
FOUNDATION STAGE	*Time to Talk* groups. Individual TA programmes planned and monitored by outside agency.		Specialist teacher works with groups. *Numicon Foundation Kit.*	Nurturing groups twice a week. *PALS* group.*	*Jump Ahead* programme with nursery nurse.
Y1	*Time to Talk* groups. Individual TA programmes planned and monitored by outside agency.	*15 minutes a day programme 1–1 with TA.* *ELS.* Guided reading and phonics groups with trained Reading Recovery teacher.	Specialist teacher works with groups. *Numicon programme.*	Nurturing groups. *PALS group.*	*Jump Ahead* programme with nursery nurse/TA.
Y2	Individual TA programmes planned and monitored by outside agency.	*15 minutes a day programme 1–1 with TA.* Guided reading and phonics groups with trained Reading Recovery teacher.	Specialist teacher works with groups. *Numicon programme.*	Nurturing groups. *Social skills groups.*	*Jump Ahead* programme with nursery nurse/TA.

Note: * **P**laying **A**nd **L**earning to **S**ocialise, www.palsprogram.com.au.

TABLE 2.6 Provision map, Tolworth Infant and Nursery School

The key to this achievement is careful tracking and target setting. This school, like Ellingham, uses Essex Target Tracker to record progress. In the early years, simple charts profile where every child is on all elements of the Foundation Stage profile; each term Rachel will look at the tracking and, together with class teachers, identify the children who are not moving up the 0–9 scales as they should be. This enables appropriate additional provision to be planned. The target-tracking software also identifies the next steps in each child's learning, breaking broad goals down into small targets.

A bank of 'I can...' statements helped to develop targets for academic, personal and social learning for all children. Targets are recorded on laminated target cards that children can keep inside their books. Teachers work alongside children to assess their achievement of targets ('You've achieved this ... and what you are going to learn next is...'). In the Foundation Stage, staff make quick notes on sticky labels as children show evidence of achieving targets, to add to their assessment profiles.

Children's progress and targets are discussed at termly meetings with parents/carers. Parents of children with SEN or disabilities will have an extra meeting once or twice a year, so that they can keep in even closer touch with how their child is doing.

CASE STUDY

3: Hall Mead School

Hall Mead School is a secondary school with 980 pupils on roll. Levels of social disadvantage are below average – just over 3 per cent of pupils are eligible for free school meals. The majority of pupils (90 per cent) are of white UK origin. One in ten pupils is identified as having SEN. Numbers of pupils with complex needs are above average; over 30 children have needs at a level that would justify a Statement. They come from the full range of backgrounds, many from professional families with articulate and knowledgeable parents who have chosen Hall Mead even though they live outside the catchment area, because of the high quality of its SEN provision.

Elizabeth, the SENCO, has been at the school for ten years. Two years ago the school decided to take part in a local authority pilot aimed at reducing the bureaucracy associated with the Statementing process.

Reducing numbers of Statements and IEPs

The school continued to make the same provision for Statemented children that it had before the pilot, and continued to access the same levels of local authority SEN funding. Parents/carers were asked, however, to agree to the local authority ceasing to maintain their child's Statement. All agreed – because, the SENCO explains, of the high level of trust they have in the school and its SEN arrangements. Once she had explained to parents that the aim of the pilot was to reduce paperwork, they could see the point and wanted to support her in the enterprise. They also knew that they would have a say in whether the pilot became permanent. At the end of the year they were asked to say whether they thought things were the same, better or worse as a result of the changes. In the event, all said that things were the same or better.

The SENCO is convinced that what matters for parents is the chance to talk to her or other staff, and not any resulting paperwork. She cites as an example her previous practice of sending home records of Statement reviews with two copies – one for parents to sign and return to the school, and one for them to keep. Invariably, they would send both copies back to the school.

Doing away with Statements has enabled the school to review its procedures for what used to be formal transition reviews. Previously these were held in the Year 9 term directed by the local authority. Now they have been rescheduled to coincide with the period when pupils are choosing their Key Stage 4 options. The SENCO books a block of time from the school's educational psychologist, Connexions adviser and other relevant professionals, so that they can meet pupils individually before their reviews. There is then a transition meeting with pupil, parents/carers and relevant professionals, which aims to make collaborative decisions about the options pupils will choose and the support that will be required. In the January of Year 11 (to coincide with dates for applications to colleges) a similar process is used to develop a 'Moving Forward' plan for post-16.

As well as reducing the numbers of Statements, Hall Mead has reviewed its policy on IEPs. The SENCO says 'I used to work very hard on IEPs but I was not sure they were helpful to teachers or relevant to the curriculum.' She also found the IEPs passed on from primary schools of limited value, as her school could not continue the intervention programmes or support in the same way. What she wanted was information on what worked for a particular child that would help secondary staff employ similar strategies.

IEPs are no longer written; instead, each child has a single-sheet profile describing their areas of difficulty and the strategies staff can adopt to the meet their needs (Table 2.7). Feeder primary schools are asked to contribute to this profile for pupils transferring.

PROFILE

M has severe visual impairment. He has good and bad seeing days although will not always say if he cannot see work.

He has a very positive attitude.

He needs specially adapted paper.

M uses a laptop.

Work written on the whiteboard should be in black.

He needs work enlarged to **at least N18.**

Simple enlargement is not always appropriate – see Sally in the learning support department. Bear in mind that some work may need to be retyped/redrawn/annotated so please allow sufficient time for work to be adapted.

He will need specially adapted SAT papers.

M's speech can be hard to understand (although this has improved).

Support needed is physical rather than academic.

STRATEGIES

Encourage M to use his laptop. His writing is hard to read (even for him) and he will need legible notes for revision. This will be good practice for GCSEs in Year 10 and 11.

He should have folders for each subject on his laptop to save his work in.

When speaking please encourage M to slow down and speak up.

Check that he can see the work you have given him.

Suitably enlarged past SAT papers are available for M to use for practice. Please liaise with the LSD as these will have to be ordered in. The LSD will be happy to adapt materials for you but please plan work in advance so that M's work is ready and suitably modified for the start of your lesson.

TABLE 2.7 Single-sheet child profile

The school no longer requests new Statements for children with the more common (high incidence) types of need. When such children transfer from primary school, there is a discussion at the transfer review meeting about arrangements at Hall Mead. Most parents are happy for the Statement to be ceased. In the first term after transfer, there will be a meeting with the child and parents/carers where the agenda is straightforward and solution-focused – how do we all think it is going, and what do we all need to do to make it go even better?

Working with subject staff

At the beginning of the year each subject department receives a folder containing the profiles of every child with SEN and disability, including children with medical needs. The folder will also contain information on the main types of SEN, on subject-specific access strategies and on general issues such as differentiation, scaffolding learning and setting homework. The first day of the year is always an INSET (in service training) day, and during the day the head of department will pull out from the folder information on the pupils in each class and arrange for each teacher to have a class set for each class they teach.

Targets for pupils with SEN are subject-specific and set by subject teachers in the context of target-setting systems for all pupils. A few pupils who need to work on life skills have additional personal plans. Subject teachers have just one sheet in their planners, called the Curriculum Access Plan (Table 2.8). It contains a list of pupils with SEN or disabilities in the class, and a space for the subject teacher to enter learning targets for the half term, term or for the module they are teaching (they choose the period that is most appropriate), and any strategies they will employ to help the pupil achieve the target. They do this only where the pupil needs adjustments made to enable them to access learning in that subject. Some pupils with SEN might not need such adjustments in music, PE or DT, for example.

Staff can also add to the list any pupil who is struggling in their subject. A child with spatial awareness difficulties, for example, might be added to the art teacher's list, with a note of strategies to be adopted to support them.

The principle used is whether or not the teacher has to *do something different* for the child to enable them to succeed in their lessons. The definition of SEN is therefore functional rather than based on labels and need types. The SENCO's message to staff is 'If they don't need anything different, then don't do a plan.'

Another principle is the need to put time and energy into frequent informal communications rather than into infrequent, formal meetings. The SENCO has a slot at the staff meeting on the first day of the school year to talk face to face to staff about particular priority pupils they should know about (such as those with autism). Specialist advisory teachers (for example, in visual impairment) also input at these meetings. The SENCO also takes

SPECIAL EDUCATION NEEDS – CURRICULUM ACCESS PLAN

FORM: 10TH Set 2/4	TEACHER: CP	DATE STARTED:	SUBJECT:

Name	Learning targets	Strategies/equipment and support details	Half-termly/Termly/ Module/Unit/Date expected to achieve by / Final outcomes with supporting comments and evidence
HM	All class targets Algebra skills of expanding, simplifying, solving, factorising to be practised and mastered. Angles on parallel lines (alternate, corresponding, interior ...).	Ensure that classwork and homework is enlarged in advance of the lesson.	
HK	Angles in polygons to be known!	Monitor H regularly – EACH lesson in case of seizures. Ensure that I read the care plan termly at least. Liaise with Mr H about any intermittent health problems. Maintain regular contact with SEN department if homework proves to be a problem.	

SPECIAL EDUCATION NEEDS – CURRICULUM ACCESS PLAN

FORM: Yr 10	TEACHER: Mr L	DATE STARTED: Autumn term	SUBJECT: Resistant Materials

Name	Learning targets	Strategies/equipment and support details	Final outcomes with supporting comments and evidence
WJ	To keep up to date with GCSE coursework. To meet deadlines.	Positive encouragement. 1-2-1 explanations where possible. Suggest discussing work with a friend to aid understanding.	
KB	As above.	As above. Nag about homework! Praise where possible.	
PJ	As above.	Give choices ... the option of avoiding sanctions	

TABLE 2.8 Curriculum Access Plans

SPECIAL EDUCATION NEEDS – CURRICULUM ACCESS PLAN

			SUBJECT: Religious Studies Half-termly/Termly/ Module/Unit/Date expected to achieve by
FORM: 8WK/Y	**TEACHER:** DH	**DATE STARTED:** October 06	

Name	Learning targets	Strategies/equipment and support details	Final outcomes with supporting comments and evidence
PJ	Knowledge and understanding of the Church, including beliefs (creed), variety (denomination), Buildings, Leadership, Worship, Ceremonies.	Check knowledge and understanding of key words. Writing frames. Homework noted correctly. Engage him 1–2–1.	
MJ	As above.	Be non-confrontational. Check knowledge and understanding of key words. Writing frames. Check knowledge and understanding of key words.	
ER	As above.	Writing frames. Engage 1 to 1. As with ER.	
CJ	As above.	Keep away from MJ and SB.	
CD	As above.		

TABLE 2.8 Continued

SPECIAL EDUCATION NEEDS – CURRICULUM ACCESS PLAN

FORM: 8WK/Y	TEACHER: HV	DATE STARTED: September 06	SUBJECT: English Half-termly/Termly/ Module/Unit/Date expected to achieve by

Name	Learning targets	Strategies/equipment and support details	Final outcomes with supporting comments and evidence
CD	He contributes regularly to class discussions. He needs to transfer this into his written work.	Encourage him to focus – seat him on his own. Have him use laptop with predictive word processor.	
CJ	To complete a formal letter to an MP using written argument phrases.	Bank of written argument phrases.	
MJ	To complete an agreed amount of work during the lesson.	Listen to his ideas. Give encouragement. Pair him with buddy for joint production of written work.	

TABLE 2.8 Continued

SPECIAL EDUCATION NEEDS – CURRICULUM ACCESS PLAN

FORM: 8A/WM	TEACHER: WM	DATE STARTED: September 06	SUBJECT: PSHE Half-termly/Termly/ Module/Unit/Date expected to achieve by
Name	Learning targets	Strategies/equipment and support details	Final outcomes with supporting comments and evidence
BS WD	To ensure he has grasped key concepts. To ensure he is on task and up to date.	See SK. Clear instructions. Move when appropriate. Involve him in discussions.	
SK	To ensure key concepts are understood (democracy, MPs, voting).	Create opportunities for work to be bullet points – simple sentences. Check each lesson that she knows what to do.	
RB	To ensure B remains confident and involved to develop written work.	Give lots of praise. Ensure there are some role-play activities.	

TABLE **2.8** Continued

advantage of the daily staff briefings to pass on information about pupils' changing situations and needs.

The school is committed to mixed ability teaching and this means staff feel a greater need for advice on how to differentiate their planning and teaching than those with setted classes. Departments prepare schemes of work with different levels of worksheet and buy textbooks at different levels. TAs are encouraged to contribute to the development of departmental resources. Departments play an active part in developing school SEN policies and practice. Each department has a nominated member of the school's learning support working party, which meets monthly to discuss SEN issues and developments. The idea of Curriculum Access Plans came from this group.

Working with parents and carers

Parents/carers are able to talk to the SENCO and her staff in the Learning Support Department when they need to rather than at set times. 'They might ring every day for a week,' Elizabeth says, 'but then not at all ... it's all about informality, easy face-to-face and telephone access, and response to need.'

The SENCO's role

The SENCO puts the majority of her time into these informal communications, and helping staff with their target setting and planning, rather than into writing or reviewing IEPs. Drop-in sessions are offered at the start of the year for teachers to get help in writing their Curriculum Access Plans. The SENCO looks at these plans and can quickly identify which departments or individuals might benefit from her input. Her monitoring of how well things are going in subject lessons is based on the informal but minuted review meetings she holds with pupils and parents/carers, and discussions with teachers and TAs.

Much time is also put into continuing professional development (CPD) for staff. There is regular INSET on SEN, involving outside agencies. There are also frequent lunchtime sessions for TAs which are open to any member of staff. Subject teachers do often bring a sandwich and join in, because the drop-ins tell them what they need to know, when they want to know it – when they are teaching a particular child who needs their help.

Elizabeth has no regrets about the move away from Statements and IEPs. She foresees further reductions in paperwork in the future, as staff become more confident in setting targets and planning for pupils with SEN in their lessons. 'You go through a paper model to get people to think in a certain way', she says, 'and then you can give the paper up when it's no longer needed.' Shortly the whole school will be moving over to electronic communication and Curriculum Access Plans will be emailed to Elizabeth, rather than having to be photocopied.

CASE STUDY

4: Coombe Boys' School

Coombe Boys' School in the London Borough of Kingston draws on a diverse community. There is a grammar school nearby that takes the most able pupils, but Coombe itself still has a spread of abilities. There are 500 11–18-year-old pupils on roll, 40 per cent of whom have English as an additional language and 22 per cent have SEN. A fifth of pupils are eligible for free school meals.

Sam Axbey, the school's INCO until 2007, formerly worked in the school's behaviour base and from that vantage point was able to observe the SEN systems in place, and their impact. 'Teachers were being given piles of IEPs and putting them in a folder never to be seen again', she says. When she became INCO she wanted to design a new system based on what teachers wanted and what they would actually use.

Layers of information

The system is based on layers of information (see Figure 2.2) – from the minimum that every teacher needs to know, down to the more detailed information that might only be needed by an outside agency working with a pupil. Information is copied only to those who need it, but also kept in a file in the staffroom so that anyone who wants to know more can access information at the more detailed level if they choose.

FIGURE 2.2 Layers of information

The first layer of information is an additional needs register containing, for each year group, the names of EAL learners and the names of pupils with SEN or disabilities together with their areas of need (BESD (behavioural, emotional and social difficulties), cognition and learning and so on) and whether they are at School Action, School Action Plus or have a Statement.

This register goes to every member of staff. It is updated termly, with changes highlighted in colour. Termly updating is necessary because the school has high levels of pupil mobility.

The next layer aims to provide teachers with more information about pupils with SEN or disabilities, but in a way that will not leave them feeling overwhelmed. It takes the form of a year group summary sheet, on no more than two sides of A4, that lists the names of pupils with SEN, the barriers to their learning, and the strategies that will be helpful (Table 2.9). Different colours identify each year group and the summary sheet is also updated termly. Copies go to teachers and to support staff.

Subject teachers have really valued this information. They highlight the names of pupils they have in their classes, and know, for example 'that one needs to sit at the front . . . that one needs to be told what he's going to be doing before he even comes in . . . this one needs to be allowed to leave the room and go to the toilet whenever he needs to'. Staff hitherto resistant to SEN ideas have particularly welcomed the new system.

The strategies on these year group summary sheets are written by the INCO and support staff. As a team, they sit down each week and discuss pupils individually, covering year groups one at a time on a rolling basis. TAs are subject-based as well as each acting as key worker for a number of pupils, so the discussions bring in perspectives of how a pupil is doing across the curriculum and the strategies that appear to work best for them. The team meetings serve a dual purpose – both generating the strategy ideas for the year group summary sheets, and providing professional development for the TAs, who are able to learn from each other's strategies and successes.

The next layer of information held on pupils, the 'individual intervention programme', is aimed at staff who are directly supporting individual pupils, either one to one or in a group, at parents/carers and outside agencies. It supplies a description of the total additional provision a pupil is receiving. Form tutors, year heads and the pupil's key worker also receive a copy.

YEAR 8		
STUDENT	BARRIERS TO LEARNING	STRATEGIES/ACTION POINTS
K 8GT MATRIX	• Behaviour. • Difficulty staying on task/focusing.	• Seat on his own at the front. • Encourage independent working. • Receives support from MB to consolidate classroom work.
S 8GT MATRIX	• Behaviour. • Low literacy.	• Has some offsite provision and is in school for partial timetable. • Buddy with a better reader in class.
E 8GT SA+	• Possible visual impairment. • Lacks confidence. • General learning difficulties.	• Seat near front.
S 8MS SA+	• Literacy – writing. • Behaviour. • Lack of confidence. • Possible dyspraxia.	• Manageable writing tasks. • Enhanced access to IT. • Emphasise S's achievements.
K 8GT SA+ EAL 1	• General learning difficulties. • Poor peer relationships.	• Responds well to praise and to explicit rewards e.g. merits. • Encourage positive peer relationships through small group work.
L 8GT SA+	• Behaviour.	• Joint placement with PRU. • Recommend speaking to social worker before speaking to mum.
D 8MS SA+	• CP issues. • Volatile behaviour. • Literacy.	• Lunchtime haven. • Focused literacy support with JB. • D to be encouraged to fully participate with other students in lessons. • Receives individual counselling.
N 8GT SA	• Literacy. • Lack of confidence. • Listening skills.	• N needs to complete small tasks in both speaking and writing.
D 8KS SA	• Young carer/home/social issues. • Low literacy levels. • Attention seeking.	• Lunchtime havens. • Acknowledge his concerns, then distract.

TABLE 2.9 Year group summary sheet

Provisions are varied and are often based on individually tailored packages – literacy programmes developed by a TA with an advanced diploma in specific learning difficulties, maths programmes with a learning support teacher, breakfast clubs to ease troubled pupils into school, residentials, college placements, sessions with a youth worker, individual swimming lessons or music tuition, group cooking sessions, one-to-one counselling and so on.

Identifying needs and working with outside agencies

Any member of staff can make a referral to the INCO, using a simple form with basic information on their concerns under Every Child Matters outcome headings that is signed off by the head of year or head of department. Referrals to outside agencies are managed by talking rather than filling in forms. Every term a whole morning is dedicated to a multi-agency review meeting attended by INCO, pastoral deputy head, heads of year and a range of outside agencies including Connexions, the Youth Offending Team, EP, school nurse and education welfare officer (EWO). Before the meeting the INCO puts together a list of pupils to be discussed and circulates it to heads of year for additions. A notice also goes up in the staffroom inviting all staff to make recommendations about students they think should be discussed. The INCO then prepares a spreadsheet, arranged by year group, with pupils' names and a space for her to add actions as they are agreed at the meeting. After the meeting she extracts a separate list of each professional's agreed actions and sends it to them.

Target setting and monitoring progress

Coombe Boys has a whole-school target-setting system based on an academic mentoring day that is held twice a year. On these days each pupil has a one-to-one meeting with their form tutor to discuss their progress and set targets for the next period. For pupils with SEN or disabilities, the key worker (usually a TA) joins the meeting to contribute feedback on progress and to help with target setting. Year heads might also sit in on meetings where there are particular behaviour or pastoral issues.

Pupils' progress is assessed termly by subject staff using National Curriculum (NC) sub-levels and each pupil receives a 'Position Statement' showing the NC level they were working towards and the level they actually reached. On the back is a graph (Figure 2.3) which totals point scores across subjects and shows progress term by term across the key stage. This is sent to parents/carers before the parents' evenings that are held twice a year.

If a referral needs to be made to the local authority for a possible Statement of SEN, or for the local system of 'Enhanced School Action Plus' funding, the INCO is able to submit the detailed pupil progress information

FIGURE 2.3 Position Statement graph

held on the Position Statement. Together with a copy of the 'layers' of information held in the staffroom file, this means that strategies, provision and outcomes are clear. None of her requests for funding have been turned down since she adopted this system.

Working with parents

Parents and carers are very closely involved in working with the school to support the progress of children with SEN or disabilities. Not one, for example, failed to come into school to meet with staff. Sam puts this down to strategies like phoning home regularly with good news, being willing to make home visits, and the messages of respect and valuing she and her staff give, summed up as 'You know your child best.' Parents supply essential information to help assess pupils' needs; Sam has devised a set of questions grouped around the five Every Child Matters outcomes that she uses for these discussions (Table 2.10).

Transfer and transition

Kingston local authority hold an annual 'transfer day' each July for primary and secondary SENCOs in the borough. Primary SENCOs come to this meeting armed with a standard transfer sheet they have completed for each pupil. The transfer sheet is a single side of A4 and has information on the pupil's type of SEN, whether SA, SA+ or Statemented, end of key stage results and extra information. Secondary SENCOs attend for the whole day,

Pupil's name ... XXX ... Does the child appear to be ...

Healthy?

> Evidence:
> Sleeps well, eats well, physically active. Eyesight fine.
> Hearing – mild hearing loss in both ears.
> No apparent worries but gets angry quite a lot at home.

Safe from harm?

> Evidence:
> Yes – but did leave the school site on one occasion unsupervised, thereby putting himself at risk.
> Says he used to get bullied but not now.

Enjoying and achieving?

> Evidence:
> No issues with learning, progress or level of attainment. Attends well – seems to like school mostly.
> However behaviour is beginning to impact on access to learning opportunities. When XXX is removed
> from class he is missing learning time.

Having a positive impact on others?

> Evidence:
> XXX's behaviour within the classroom can have a negative impact on other children and their access
> to learning.
> Has been involved in providing reading support to Y7 – really successful.

Heading for a good future?

> Needs help in working out what sort of future he wants. Can be a leader. Working in teams is
> something he struggles with. Good at taking responsibility and has lots of creative ideas.

TABLE 2.10 Assessment used in discussions with parents/carers

so that their primary colleagues can pass on the transfer sheets and discuss particular pupils. The system is being expanded to include vulnerable pupils and pupils with behaviour issues.

Transition to life after school is also carefully managed in the borough. The INCO and year head are able to refer any pupil at risk of leaving school with no destination for targeted support over the course of Year 11, and Coombe has very close links with its Connexions careers adviser and, for its most vulnerable pupils, with Connexions personal advisers.

3 Doing SEN Differently

The case studies: common features

What can we learn from the schools, described in the previous chapter, who have chosen to 'do SEN differently' and less bureaucratically? First, we can note that none of the schools over-identify pupils as having SEN. Numbers identified in the schools with lower levels of deprivation are around 10–12 per cent of the school roll, rather than the 18–19 per cent average that applies across the country.

As numbers of pupils identified as having SEN continue to grow nationally, it is a good time for schools to review how and why they are placing pupils on the SEN register. Can it really be, for example, that nearly one in three nine-year-old boys have SEN? This is what their teachers now think, according to official figures (DCSF, 2007b). We know why this happens. Pressures to achieve ever higher standards encourage teachers to attribute the lack of success of some children to within-child deficits; CVA results look better if high numbers of children ostensibly have SEN; children can have extra time in their end of key stage tests if they have SEN, and so on. But if your school is placing more than 10 per cent of pupils on its register, it may be worth discussing the resulting bureaucratic demands on everyone's time (to the detriment of time spent teaching), or at the very least making it a policy that for only some of the children you place on the register will there be an expectation of individual planning and record keeping.

Second, even if you reduce the numbers identified as having SEN to a relatively low percentage of your roll, you may also want to learn from the case study schools described in Chapter 2 and as far as possible use **the ordinary systems in place for all pupils** to establish targets for pupils with SEN, to track their progress and to communicate progress to parents and carers. This is the feature that characterises all the case study schools, who were able to take advantage of existing paper systems (pupil Learning Logs, teacher mark books, medium- and short-term planning documents) rather than set up separate paper trails for pupils with SEN.

This has benefits beyond reducing bureaucracy. It locates much of the responsibility with the class or subject teachers – those who are in greatest contact with the pupil and therefore have the greatest influence on their learning – rather than with the SENCO or learning support department. It means that teachers keep pupils' targets and the strategies required to meet them in their minds, because they are embedded in planning tools and records that are in daily use. It makes a reality of the commitment in both the SEN Code of Practice and the government's ten-year strategy for SEN, *Removing barriers to achievement* (DfES, 2004d), that 'every teacher is a teacher of SEN'.

It is not, however, what a literal adherence to the SEN Code of Practice has led us to. For many years, such adherence has placed a whole group of children outside of schools' regular systems for setting expectations, monitoring progress and reviewing and adapting curriculum, organisation and teaching methods. Pupils with SEN were felt to require **different** systems from the systems used to secure the welfare and progress of all pupils.

This has rarely been helpful. Ofsted, for example, notes that:

> Defining achievement in terms of the number of targets on an individual education plan achieved across a given time rarely ensured rigorous evaluation of provision or pupils' progress. What made the difference to higher outcomes was effective target-setting within the curriculum or personalised programme as part of a whole-school policy on assessment.
>
> (Ofsted, 2006a)

Abandoning separate SEN systems, however, also carries distinct risks. At the extreme, it could mean that the particular needs of pupils with SEN or disabilities get lost – that teachers are unaware of their needs, that no special efforts are made to teach them in the ways they learn best, that additional provision is not made for them; and that parents are left in the dark about what the school is doing to help their child.

The aim of this book is to show how these pitfalls can be avoided. It will describe how we can 'do SEN differently', whilst never losing track of the essential purposes of SEN and disability legislation and guidance – protecting the rights of a minority group of children to have their needs identified and met.

The functions that SEN procedures were meant to fulfil

To ensure that the rights of children and parents are protected, we need first to reflect on the intended purposes of the SEN Code of Practice.

These include:

- Identification – ensuring that children's needs are identified as a result of expressions of concern by teachers or parent/carers.
- Assessment – ensuring that some assessment takes place, to better understand the barriers to learning and how they might be overcome.
- Communication – making sure that all relevant staff and outside agencies know what the child's needs are and what should be done or has been done to support them.
- Identifying priorities and setting targets for learning or behaviour.
- Planning strategies, in the classroom and elsewhere, to help the child achieve targets.
- Reviewing progress and celebrating success.
- Engaging parents and carers – agreeing priorities and targets with them, making sure that they know what is being done to help their child and to what effect, suggesting ways in which they can support their child's progress.
- Coordinating the actions to be taken by the school and outside agencies.
- Informing decisions about the allocation of resources – extra adult time and/or physical resources.
- Supporting transition – making sure that information about the child's needs is passed on as they move from one class or setting to another.

Other less intrinsically useful but necessary functions of the staged procedures of the SEN Code are those of accountability and referral:

- Proving to parents, tribunals, Ofsted and the local authority that the school is meeting pupils' needs effectively.
- Demonstrating a need for additional resources (the involvement of outside agencies, extra funding) by showing that the school has done all it reasonably can before seeking outside help.

Let us now take each of these functions in turn, and consider ways of fulfilling them that are manageable, effective and non-bureaucratic, taking our case studies from Chapter 2 as the starting point.

Identification and assessment

All the schools in our case studies employed sophisticated *pupil tracking* (moderated by sensible teacher and parent judgement) to identify children causing concern. They all then kept some sort of register of pupils flagged up in this way – thus meeting this particular Code of Practice function.

Ideally, their pupil-tracking systems could be supplemented by routine screening to identify children who may on the face of it be making adequate progress yet are not fulfilling their potential or secure in their well-being. These will be children who have special needs of a more subtle, less obvious kind. The SENCO/INCO might, for example, ask year group teams once a year to look through checklists of indicators of dyslexia, autistic spectrum disorder, dyspraxia and minor sensory impairment, and consider whether any of the children in their care show evidence of these potential special needs.

Equally, SENCOs/INCOs might want to enhance their school's assessment systems by providing training to colleagues (class teachers, form tutors or the personal tutors that have been suggested for all pupils) on how to conduct assessment interviews with children. Such interviews should help them identify a pupil's strengths, the barriers they experience to their learning, and what helps them overcome these barriers. SENCOs/INCOs might in addition want to spend some of the time freed up from paperwork working with individual pupils, using tools suggested by outside agencies, so as to develop a more in-depth picture of the child's cognitive, physical or social/emotional profile that can guide curriculum planning.

 ## Communicating needs

One of the prime functions that IEPs were meant to fulfil was that of communication, for example, making sure that:

- staff teaching a child were aware of their needs, targets and the strategies to be deployed;
- parents/carers were involved and were updated regularly on the child's progress;
- if the child failed to make progress, information on what had been done

to help them would be available for outside agencies and the local authority;

- if the child moved, information would follow them to a new placement.

In practice, the volume of IEPs that many schools maintain has made them unviable as an effective communication tool. As we saw in Chapter 2, they often languish in the drawers of the primary class teacher, or in the drawers of the learning support department in secondary schools, brought out only when accountability – in the shape of Ofsted or IEP review dates – looms. Parental involvement in many schools is reduced to token status, with the class teacher or SENCO pursuing a parent in the playground to ask them to sign an IEP in which they have had no part, simply so that it can be forwarded to the local authority to prove the case for additional resources. Paperwork is passed on to other schools if the pupil moves, but does not always tell them what they need to know and know quickly – what are this child's strengths and difficulties, what works for them in the classroom, and what additional provision they require.

There are, however, simple and more effective ways in which the IEP communication function can be met, that do not require volumes of paper. The case studies in Chapter 2 exemplify good, non-bureaucratic practice in communicating with staff, parents/carers and the outside world. At Ellingham, a child-held Communication Passport serves to summarise needs and the strategies required to meet them. At Hall Mead and Coombe, subject teachers receive customised lists of pupils they teach who have SEN or disabilities, in the form of a set of individual profiles, or a year group summary sheet.

Other schools maintain a profile of pupil need in each class that a subject teacher will work with by creating pupil profiles that are short enough to fit into one cell of a spreadsheet (Table 3.1). They then sort the profiles into class sets electronically.

And why stick to paper? A secondary SENCO in Bristol took a video camera out and interviewed Year 6 pupils with SEN or disabilities who were due to come to his school. He asked them what helped them learn and what got in the way of their learning. A hearing-impaired child with good lip-reading skills described how 'I can't manage when two people talk at once', and 'It's really bad when the teacher talks when they are writing on the board 'cos I can't see what they are saying.' Shown to all subject staff who were to

> Morris, Joanne. Excellent at art. Plays for school netball team. Learning difficulties. Reads at level of an 8 yr old. Numeracy similar. Needs a buddy reader, short instructions, writing frames, learning linked to everyday real experiences. Can get very upset/difficult when falls out with friends – show understanding and ask her if it would help to go and talk to Miss Perry.

TABLE 3.1 A cell from a spreadsheet

teach the incoming Year 7, these short films were far more powerful in changing teacher behaviour than any number of written communications.

There is no logical reason, either, why communication systems that let staff know about children's special needs or disabilities should not extend to wider 'additional needs'. One primary school uses 21 'special categories of need' which include 'children who do not shine in anything' and 'children who receive minimal support at home to achieve basic skills'. Children are evaluated against these categories and efforts then made to tailor provision to the need. Other schools operate a 'risk and resilience' system. They keep a list of 'at risk' pupils that might include a range of factors – being a summer-born boy, living in a home where there is domestic violence, parental separation, poverty, and so on. They alert staff to pupils on this register and suggest a range of strategies that could promote the pupils' resilience – for example, all members of staff having the names of two pupils they will make a point of chatting to in the corridors and around the school each week, offering residential opportunities and before- and after-school clubs, or linking the pupil with a member of staff who shares an interest they have.

 ## Identifying priorities and setting targets

As the case study schools in Chapter 2 illustrate, setting individual targets is now commonplace, whether they are recorded on Learning Logs (as at Ellingham), laminated cards in children's books (as at Tolworth) or teachers' planning (as at Hall Mead). This meets the purposes of the SEN Code and removes the need for a separate IEP system, as long as progress against targets is systematically recorded and parents kept informed.

Where more effort may be needed for children with SEN is in making sure that the right priorities have been established for the child's learning, even before targets are set. These priorities may not always be in the core academic subjects. Underpinning areas such as language development or social and emotional learning may be more important. This though is not just an SEN issue – teachers have to judge priorities carefully for many children, including those going through a difficult time at home, those learning English as an additional language, and so on. Schools will be good at setting the right priorities to the extent that they have robust systems for gathering information on all their pupils, listening to parents/carers and listening to children and young people themselves.

 ## Planning strategies to meet needs and reach targets

The SENCOs/INCOs in our case study schools all spend considerable time on staff development, so that teachers have a good sense of how to make their everyday teaching as inclusive as they can. On top of this, they provide class and subject teachers with suggested strategies for individual pupils. At Ellingham these strategies can be found on the laminated Communication Passport, framed in the child's own language. At Tolworth, they can be found on classroom walls. At the secondary schools they are on year group summary sheets or in a folder of individual profiles for each class. Essentially, the role of the SENCO/INCO and their team in these schools has switched from paper manager to acting as a consultant to colleagues on what works for lower-attaining pupils or those with behavioural, emotional and social difficulties.

The second way in which the case study schools record the strategies employed to help pupils meet targets is through provision maps. These set out the additional provision made in each year group under the broad areas of literacy, mathematics, language, motor skills and social/emotional development. A map highlighted with the provision a particular pupil receives, together with guidance for staff on strategies to adopt in everyday class teaching, fulfils the planning strategies function of the SEN Code effectively in a time-saving way, obviating the need to keep writing the same descriptions of provision over and over again on separate IEPs.

 ## Reviewing progress and celebrating success

Once strategies have been planned, monitoring progress is readily achieved through the excellent tracking systems in place in our case study schools.

These schools also have a means of *evaluating* progress that was never available under the IEP system. Provision mapping enables schools to use simple baseline measures before an intervention is put in, and repeat these at the end of the intervention. These may be measures of reading or spelling age, standardised scores on a maths test, measures of social and emotional competence or simply teacher-assessed NC sub-levels. The measures allow not only for the progress of individuals to be evaluated (and shared with parents), but also for evaluation of the overall impact of the intervention on a number of pupils.

Children who experience barriers to their learning often need more effort put into the celebration of success than do their peers. IEP review meetings sometimes provided for this. To make sure that this celebration function is not lost, schools can flag up some children for extra 'noticing'. In secondary schools, this may be achieved by asking staff to send good news home – to make a note in a pupil's planner or send a pre-printed card home when the pupil has met a target, however small. It may be more frequent meetings between a pupil and a tutor or mentor, to review what has been achieved. In primary schools, home-school diaries and good-news postcards can also be used, along with praise assemblies, class plenaries and so on.

 ## Engaging parents and carers

A prime function of the SEN Code was to provide parents and carers with guaranteed involvement in the school's efforts to meet their child's needs, and a way of challenging the school if these efforts were insubstantial. In practice, this function has been poorly fulfilled by bureaucratic systems. In contrast, the relatively paper-free systems at our case study schools are partnered by conspicuous efforts to engage parents and carers. This is achieved in different ways at each school. What characterises them all is informality and ease of access. Extra time is given at parents' evenings where children have additional needs (as at Ellingham); meetings are more frequent (as at Tolworth), or the school has drop-in sessions and identifies a key link person for parents to speak to whenever they need to. The additional provision that can be made for their child is made clear to parents through a provision map that describes different interventions and provision, and what entry levels entitle a child to access that provision.

IEPs and reviews were also meant to enlist the help of parents in supporting their child's learning at home, and supply guidance on how best to go about this. Again, as we will see in Chapter 8, they have rarely achieved this. What does seem to be both successful and time-efficient, however, is practice like that at Ellingham, where parents are involved in curriculum workshops and support groups that are explicitly aimed at empowering them to furnish the best possible home learning environment.

 ## Coordinating the actions to be taken by the school and outside agencies

Where a number of agencies are involved with a pupil there is a need for a system that coordinates and records their work. Some schools may wish to continue using IEPs where several different agencies are involved with a pupil. Equally effective, however, in recording who is going to do what (and when) can be a simple note of actions agreed in multi-agency meetings. This is the system at Coombe Boys' School in our case studies. And to keep an overall perspective of which agencies and personnel have been involved over time, the SENCO/INCO can add a column labelled 'external agency involvement' to the school's provision map and write in the agencies involved when pulling off a copy and highlighting provision that an individual pupil receives. Alternatively, the agency involvement can be recorded on a chart like the one in Table 3.2, or the cumulative overview/record of progress which will be described in Chapter 5.

 ## Informing decisions about the allocation of resources

The SEN Code was intended to make sure that schools allocate resources according to pupil need, basing decisions on staged procedures in which progressively more resources are allocated as pupils move from School Action to Action Plus or a Statement. The theory is that, if the resources deployed at one stage are not successful in helping the pupil progress, more resources are needed. In practice, the staged system has often served only to distort efficient management of time and money. It still drives much of the excess paperwork schools undertake, as they seek to document in detail what has been done at each stage so as to make a case for a move to the next. It assumes that, if resource allocation has been unsuccessful, then the *child* must have needs greater than those resources could support. It does not prompt schools to consider whether they have deployed resources effectively in the first place. Nor does it lead to equity. Several pieces of research have now shown (Gross, 1996; Pinney, 2004) that resources tend

Child: xxxxxxxxxx   **DOB: 21.02.99**   **Class: 3R**

Updated: March 2007

Foundation Stage intervention group – numeracy	Foundation Stage intervention group – literacy	Hearing impairment team support	Visual impairment team support	TA supported literacy 1:1
TA supported numeracy 1:1	Handwriting programme	Speech and language therapy	Language group	RML
Specialist literacy support	Learning Support unit	Learning mentor	CAMHS	Educational psychologist
EMAG support	1st language assessment	Lang. & communication team	Behaviour support	Child development team
Stephen Hawkins Special School Outreach team advice	Liaison with Phoenix Special School	Statement provision	Physical disability team	IEP
IBP	Occupational therapy	Daily physiotherapy	PSP	Medical intervention
CT-supported writing group	1:1 maths with TA			

Past provisions   Present provision

TABLE 3.2 Record of provision and multiagency involvement, Old Ford Primary School

to be skewed towards those children whose parents are most able to articulate the case for extra help.

The schools in our case studies tend to use more effective ways of allocating resources. These are based on data analysis that identifies the level and type of need in each year group. On the basis of this analysis, provision is planned proactively, at the start of the year, then regularly adjusted through pupil-tracking systems that quickly identify pupils who are not making the expected progress.

Supporting transition

Another purpose of the SEN Code was to secure the effective exchange of information at times of transition for pupils – moving from one class to another, or from one school to another. Our case study schools have not found that the transfer of copies of individual paper plans is helpful.

Instead, they allocate time for primary and secondary staff to meet, as at Coombe Boys', or explicitly ask for information on the strategies that worked in the primary school, as at Hall Mead. Another useful idea for primary schools is the class handover profile you will find in the Toolkit section of this book. Some schools also have an end-of-year staff meeting, where staff team up in pairs (Year R with Year 1, etc.) and go through class lists, discussing particular children's needs, what has worked for them in the past, what triggers to avoid, and any other relevant information. The pair record a profile for each child discussed and photocopy it there and then for the SENCO/INCO and the teacher whose class the child will be joining.

 ## Proving that the school is meeting pupils' needs effectively or demonstrating a need for additional resources

This is the big worry for many schools. How, without drawers full of IEPs and fat pupil files containing dusty records of what is often years of SEN support, can a school show Ofsted that their practice is good, convince a SEN tribunal that they have acted appropriately; request the involvement of outside agencies, or compile evidence so as to request a Statement of SEN?

Let us look first at Ofsted. At a recent inspection, the SENCO was asked to select a number of children and show their 'value-added' progress over the key stage, and what had been done to support them. At another, the SENCO was asked for records of meetings with parents and the IEPs that went with them. At another, the focus was on how the SENCO could show the overall impact of the school's SEN provision on pupil progress.

On the face of it, some of these inspectors could be seen to be asking for paperwork. But they asked for it not so as to tick a 'paperwork-in-order box', but so as to explore particular issues and hypotheses. The issues and hypotheses will have emerged from the school's data profile, from their study of the school's self-evaluation form (SEF), and from firsthand evidence earlier in the inspection.

In the school where the SENCO was asked to show the progress of individuals over time and what had been done to support them, there might have been an indication in the SEF that pupils with SEN or disabilities as a group were not making good progress.

In the school where documentation of meetings with parents was the apparent focus, the inspectors may have picked from questionnaires broader issues about parental involvement and satisfaction, and decided to explore whether these issues extended to parents of pupils with SEN or disabilities.

In the school where the SENCO was asked how she could show the impact of the school's provision, the inspectors might have been testing a hypothesis about leadership and management, having noted an absence of any data analysis relating to the progress of lower-attaining pupils, and any evaluation of the impact of the school's interventions for pupils with additional needs.

In all cases, Ofsted was not interested in compliance with procedures. Its interest was in outcomes – pupils' academic and personal development, and in what the school was or was not doing to help pupils achieve these outcomes. In some cases it did look for evidence in the paper systems that are generally used; inspectors did go to the familiar (to IEPs and reviews) because that is where they would expect to find evidence.

But they can equally be directed to other forms of evidence. It is up to the school to point them in the right direction. The SENCO/INCO can do this by writing a single sheet, part of their SEN or inclusion policy, that describes how the needs of children with SEN are met – the systems for identification, assessment, setting targets, identifying strategies, working with parents/carers, involving pupils and so on. The sheet will make it clear for which children the school uses IEPs (for example, those with the most complex needs) and those for whom it employs alternative means of planning. It will give the rationale for the systems that are in operation, so that the reader understands the benefits that result from reduced bureaucracy and increased class/subject teacher involvement.

An example of such a policy statement is provided in the toolkit section of this book. Suitably adapted, this information sheet can be given to inspectors so that they will know where they need to look in order to test out the effectiveness of the school's work with pupils who have learning difficulties or disabilities. In the examples above, they would be pointed to these sources of information:

Progress of individuals over time	⇨	Class tracking sheets and provision map
Parental involvement and satisfaction	⇨	Twice-yearly reports for parents and notes of meetings
The impact of the school's provision	⇨	Data analysis showing the number of NC level jumps made by all the pupils with SEN over a key stage. Evaluations of interventions on provision map

All of these would provide fruitful ground for testing of inspectorial hypotheses, whilst at the same time demonstrating that this is a school that has thought carefully about how to develop truly effective systems for supporting pupils with additional needs.

Another big fear for schools, which often drives unnecessary bureaucracy, is the fear of being called to account by parents through tribunals or the courts. As the Implementation Review Group of headteachers puts it, 'Too often we are driven by what appears to be the overriding concern of protection from litigation' (IRU, 2006). But, just as for Ofsted, similar 'evidence' (this time solely at the individual pupil level) can easily be pulled together from existing sources to demonstrate what has been done to support a pupil. At tribunals, the focus is likely to be on the provision map and evidence of strategies deployed by class or subject teachers (like the Curriculum Access Plans in the case studies) as the questions will usually be about what provision the school can make available, and whether this is sufficient. Similar issues will be of interest in any court procedures.

Finally, in relation to outside agencies, it is not difficult to deliver succinct information about the child's needs and what has been done so far to meet them, through:

● Personal Profiles or Communication Passports;
● pupil-tracking records showing progress in NC levels and sub-levels and in personal development;
● highlighted provision maps.

If further 'proof' is needed, for example when requesting a statutory assessment, then photocopies of records of class-based target setting and review, and of differentiated classroom planning, can also be appended. Again, you may need to include your information sheet on how you manage SEN in your school, so that the agency or local authority administrators will understand that you haven't just forgotten to enclose 'copies of the last three IEPs' or whatever else their own bureaucracy asks for, but are supplying the same information in a different way.

Beating bureaucracy: the essential kit

A simple set of systems will allow you both to provide information to others who ask for it, and at the same time manage SEN effectively internally. We can call this the essential bureaucracy-busting kit. It is illustrated in the toolkit section of this book and should include:

- a note in your SEN policy on how you fulfil the functions of the Code of Practice without over-reliance on IEPs, as described in the previous section;
- a register of pupils with SEN;
- a provision map to show what additional provision you are making for pupils;
- a pupil-led way of communicating needs to all who work with the pupil, such as a Personal Profile or Communication Passport;
- strategy sheets for the main types of SEN, to highlight and give to staff;
- a way of differentiating curriculum planning;
- a way of tracking pupil progress and reporting regularly to parents/carers.

The **register** is needed so that you can complete your pupil census (PLASC), identify the percentage of your roll with SEN, and make links to the range of data the school holds on each pupil. Without a register you cannot define the group whose progress you will want, as SENCO/INCO, to evaluate and compare with that of pupils not on the SEN register. The simplest way of keeping a register is to use an existing information management system, such as SIMS or RAISEonline, recording a 'Yes' in School Action, School Action Plus or Statement columns and the type of SEN in another column. You can then print your register, if you need to, using the filtering function.

The **provision map,** described in Chapter 7, is fundamentally a planning tool for you but also, when copied, dated and highlighted to show the provision received by an individual child, serves as a record of what the school has done to provide support.

The **Personal Profile** or **Communication Passport** helps staff identify individual pupils' strengths and barriers to learning, and what helps them best.

Strategy sheets give handy hints on strategies for specific types of SEN (dyslexia, autistic spectrum disorder, speech and language difficulties, ADHD and so on). They can be copied, highlighted as appropriate for the individual pupil, and given to staff who work with the child.

A **system for differentiating curriculum planning** is the way that staff translate information from Personal Profiles and strategy sheets into learning and teaching in the classroom.

Reporting to parents can be done through written reports and meetings. For children with SEN, there will need to be additional agenda items, over and above those in standard parents' meetings, plus a brief record of the key points of discussion at meetings, and any actions agreed.

Summary

In this chapter we have considered systems that can be adopted to fulfil the purposes of current SEN procedures, and the essential toolkit to support these less bureaucratic ways of working. Table 3.3 overleaf affords an overview of the purposes of current procedures, and the alternative ways of fulfilling them. In subsequent chapters we will return to these headings and consider some of them in more detail.

Purpose of Code of Practice	Alternative ways of fulfilling these purposes	Beating bureaucracy toolkit
To ensure that children's needs are identifiedthrough the f expression oconcern by parents/carers or teachers.	• Effective tracking of pupil progress. • Screening procedures (for example, for dyslexia), described in SEN policy.	SEN register derived from SIMS or other school information management systems.
To encourage a thorough assessment of the factors which may be contributingto a child's difficulties.	• SENCO trains/coaches colleagues (in primary schools class teachers, in secondary schools form tutors or personal tutors) in involving the pupil in identifying strengths, difficulties and what helps. • Use of information from outside agencies' assessments.	Regular school conferencing systems.
To ensure that all relevant staff and outside agencies know what the child's needs are.	• Pupil-held personal profiles that record strengths, difficulties and what helps. • Training for pupils in how to communicate their needs.	Personal Profile or Communication Passport.
To help staff and pupils identify key priorities and learning targets.	• Pupil-owned targets set together by the class or subject teacher and the pupil.	Regular whole-school systems for setting individual targets.
To ensure that effective strategies are put in place to support the child.	• Strategy sheets for staff. • SENCO or school-based behaviour/SEAL specialist acts as consultant to colleagues on what works for lower attaining pupils and those with behavioural, emotional and social difficulties.	Regular whole-school systems for differentiated curriculum planning. Strategy sheets. Provision map.
To review progress and celebrate success.	Assessments used before and after an intervention; effective tracking systems that use NC levels and sublevels; intensification of regular school systems for awards and celebrations.	Regular whole-school tracking and review systems. Intervention data collection system.

TABLE 3.3 Overview of current procedures

To ensure that parents/carers know what is being done to help their child, and to what effect.	• School SEN policy/ School Profile contains clear provision map showing the extra provision and what entry levels entitle a child to access that provision.	Provision map. Additional agenda items for progress review meetings with parents and pupils.
To ensure that parents/carers know what they can do to help their child.	• Communicating pupils' progress to parents/carers at least twice a year. • SENCO and curriculum specialists run workshops for parents/families and implement projects (such as paired reading) for specified groups.	
To coordinate the actions to be taken by the school and outside agencies.	A column added to provision map, or agency involvement recorded on a single cumulative overview/record of progress.	Provision map. Cumulative overview/record of progress.
To ensure that school resources are effectively deployed.	Planning additional provision through a provision map.	Provision map.
To ensure continuity at times of transition.	Teacher/school passes on pupil personal profile and record of additional provision (highlighted, dated provision maps).	Personal profile or Communication Passport. Provision map.
To demonstrate what has been done at school level before seeking r support ofunding from outside agencies/local authority.	SENCO/INCO provides copy of extract from school SEN policy on how it fulfils the functions of the Code of Practice without over-reliance on IEPs. They highlight on school's provision map the extra provision the child has received. They send outcomes of regular tracking of progress, examples of differentiated classroom planning, pupil personal profile.	Provision map. Personal Profile/Communication Passport. Photocopied regular curriculum planning and tracking.

Personalised Learning and SEN

The last chapter looked at alternative ways of meeting the core functions of the SEN Code of Practice, ways that rely primarily on the application of systems meant for all children, rather than separate systems for a few. These alternatives are closely linked to developments in the education system that come under the banner of 'personalisation' or 'personalised learning'. In this chapter we will draw out the links between new SEN systems and personalisation, and consider the role of the SENCO/INCO in supporting personalisation in their school.

What is personalised learning?

The idea of personalised learning has been around for some time. It originated as a political concept, designed to capture voters' desire for services that recognise and respond to them as individuals. In the private sector, this might mean banking as it used to be many years ago, when people had a bank manager who knew their name and circumstances, spoke to them face to face or on the phone, responded to their unique financial needs – the antithesis of that feeling of being a faceless account number, of pressing numbers on a phone but never speaking to a real person, of getting irritating standard letters that aren't quite right for your particular situation. In the health sector, it might mean seeing and being known by the same doctor rather than a series, of being a person not a 'case' or a set of notes. In education, the personalisation message tapped parents' wish for something other than a 'bog-standard' education in a large and impersonal school no different from a thousand others.

An early definition of personalisation in the education system suggested that:

> To make excellence and fairness for all a reality, we have to build every aspect of education around the individual pupil. This means an end to the one-size-fits-all system, where too many pupils – particularly from poorest backgrounds – slipped through the net.

Every child is different, with their own unique talents and abilities. This means designing assessment, teaching, curriculum and school strategies around the needs of learners, welcoming support from families and wider communities.

(Charles Clarke, Headteachers' conference, 20 November 2003)

Translating political ideas into education practice is not always easy, but a number of educationalists, notably Professor David Hopkins, began to map what personalisation might look like in practice. A variety of components were seen as fundamental – curriculum design, school organisation, providing learning that extends beyond the school context into the local community and beyond, and the use of ICT to tailor learning to the individual. Indeed, personalisation seemed to have so many components that it embraced everything a good school might do for its learners.

A key element in everyone's definitions was assessment for learning. The process of assessment for learning (shown in Figure 4.1) has been described by such writers as Black *et al.* (2003) and Clarke (2001).

Later government guidance on personalisation (DfES, 2005b) described it as 'the key to tackling the persistent achievement gaps between different social and ethnic groups. It means a tailored education for every child and young

FIGURE 4.1 Process of assessment for learning

person, that gives them strength in the basics, stretches their aspirations, and builds their life chances.' Components this time were defined as:

- extra small group or one-to-one tuition for those that need it, not as a substitute for excellent whole-class teaching, but as an integrated part of the child's learning;
- opportunities for all children to get extra support and tuition in subjects and activities that they are interested in, as well as access to a range of opportunities beyond the school day, including weekend and holiday courses and online learning;
- exciting whole-class teaching, which gets the best from every child;
- setting or grouping children of similar ability and attainment together;
- a rich, flexible and accessible curriculum and, for older pupils, one that allows them to mix academic and vocational learning; and
- innovative use of ICT, both in the classroom and to link the classroom and home.

This definition set the scene for a policy direction based on allocating extra funds for catch-up tuition for individuals and groups – sometimes clearly targeted at the 'cusp' groups, who with just a little help can get back to age-expected levels, but more recently at **all** who are not making progress, including the very lowest-achieving children.

Personalisation developments

Personalisation soon began to be built into all sorts of new developments in education. When Planning, Preparation and Assessment (PPA) time was first introduced, it was intended that teachers use it to personalise their lessons, planning study programmes to suit each individual child. Personalised planning was to be based on careful tracking of pupils' progress, with performance data collected and analysed by teachers every term so as to quickly identify individuals and groups not on track to achieve the long-term numerical targets set for them.

Personalisation has also been built into how schools describe themselves, and how they are evaluated and held to account. The school profile, for example, must have a section on how the school makes sure that 'Every child receives teaching to meet their individual needs'. School improvement partners must ask the question 'What evidence is there that the school is tailoring the curriculum on offer and teaching and learning to the particular needs of individual pupils?'

Teachers in training are meant to learn about personalisation: the Teacher Development Agency's revised standards for achieving qualified teacher status (QTS) (2007) require that trainees 'have a knowledge and understanding of a range of teaching, learning and behaviour management strategies and how to use and adapt them, including how to personalise learning and provide opportunities for all learners to achieve their potential'. Personalised learning is here defined as 'maintaining a focus on individual progress, in order to maximise all learners' capacity to learn, achieve and participate.... Personalising learning is not about individual lesson plans or individualisation (where learners are taught separately or largely through a one-to-one approach).'

Despite widespread use, there remained some confusion about what the term personalised learning actually meant in practice, and what its implications might be for the schools of the future. Anxious to achieve greater clarity, the government set up a review group to establish a vision of what personalised teaching and learning might look like in schools in 2020.

In their report (DfES, 2006g) the review group, led by Christine Gilbert, put forward the following definition:

> Put simply, personalising learning and teaching means taking a highly structured and responsive approach to each child and young person's learning, in order that all are able to progress, achieve and participate. It means strengthening the link between learning and teaching by engaging pupils – and their parents – as partners in learning.

A strategy for personalising learning, the review group concludes, means:

- Using data and assessment information rigorously, together with knowledge of factors that might influence pupils' progress, to shape teaching and assess its impact.
- Matching high quality teaching to the different and developing abilities of pupils, focused on breaking down barriers to learning and progress and underpinned by high expectations.
- Regular monitoring of progress and rapid responses at the point at which pupils begin to fall behind, so that there is a relentless focus on pupils 'keeping up'.
- Dialogue between teachers and pupils, encouraging pupils to explore their ideas through talk, to ask and answer questions, to listen to their

teachers and peers, to build on the ideas of others and to reflect on what they have learnt.

- Collaborative relationships which encourage and enable all pupils to participate and which develop pupils' skills of working independently and in groups, enabling teachers and pupils to move learning forward together.
- Judicious use of whole-class teaching, as well as one-to-one, paired and group work.
- Using more open-ended tasks with pupils, either individually or in groups, based on specific projects or areas of inquiry.
- Developing pupils' appetite for and attitude to lifelong learning.

There is an insistence that 'all pupils, not just the gifted and talented or those who are having difficulties, should receive 1–1 attention focused on their learning', and a strong emphasis on pupils taking ownership of learning (Figure 4.2).

Implications for pupils with SEN or disabilities

Much of the rhetoric of personalised learning describes elements already embodied in good SEN practice. Pupil involvement in setting targets and reviewing progress, one-to-one attention, extra tuition, a flexible curriculum, the use of ICT, and individually planned study programmes are all things that many SEN practitioners would say are core to their work.

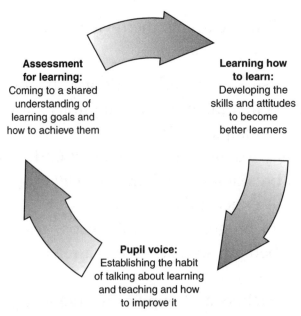

Assessment for learning:
Coming to a shared understanding of learning goals and how to achieve them

Learning how to learn:
Developing the skills and attitudes to become better learners

Pupil voice:
Establishing the habit of talking about learning and teaching and how to improve it

FIGURE 4.2 Taking ownership of learning

What is happening now, however, is that there is an intention to spread these practices to all children rather than just the few with identified SEN. And giving schools and teachers responsibility for personalised learning for **all** pupils means that many of the separate processes described in the SEN Code of Practice will become subsumed into teachers' everyday classroom practice.

The requirement that pupils with SEN, and only pupils with SEN, should have individual targets that are monitored and reviewed (with the involvement of parents/carers and the pupil) will become less and less relevant.

This is made explicit in a government consultation document *Making good progress* (DfES, 2007):

> The personalised classroom does not entail having up to 30 separate teaching plans; it is about having one strong inclusive teaching plan which allows as much room as possible for individual engagement, targeted support, a degree of choice and respect for the range of abilities and interests in the class. In the personalised classroom, it is recognised that all children have individual learning needs, not just those with Special Educational Needs.

The Gilbert review goes so far as to suggest that every child has an individual learning plan, developed by an adult who works with them to agree individual targets for their learning, and monitors progress across a range of indicators including personal, social and learning-to-learn skills. In primary schools, the class teacher would take this role; in secondary schools a new role, that of 'learning guide, is suggested – someone who understands the pupil's learning needs across subjects and meets them at least half termly (or more often for vulnerable pupils) for an extended formal review session. The learning guide (now called a 'personal tutor' by the DCSF) would also have responsibility for understanding wider factors impacting on pupils' learning and would draw on resources or other specialist guidance and support in order to help them make progress.

What is suggested here, and is already in place in many schools, is a *universal* system for identifying individual needs and acting on them.

We could envisage SEN practice as simply bringing to bear on these universal systems a particular expertise in SEN and disability, provided by the SENCO/INCO and outside agencies. This would represent an intensification of existing systems rather than instigating separate ones, and locate action within everyday classroom teaching and learning rather than a parallel universe of separate SEN record keeping and review.

This idea of progressive intensification was expressed by the House of Commons Education and Skills Select Committee in its 2006 report on SEN.

> To achieve real progress in terms of early intervention the Government needs to change the premise on which SEN is provided to one in which literally every child matters. This would mean a radically new approach to SEN provision where a system of assessment of learning and intervention takes place for every child on a spectrum of provision that can be geared up for children that require high levels of support.

The SENCO/INCO's role in personalisation: an example

In a personalised education system, we have suggested, the role of the SENCO/INCO should be to apply their particular knowledge of SEN and disabilities so as to scale up existing personalised systems in place for all children. Let us look at one example to see how that might work in practice. The example chosen is the interaction between personalisation and the identification and assessment of needs element of the SEN Code of Practice procedures.

There will always be children who come to school with needs that have already been identified – children with developmental disorders or impairments evident before they started school, or children who move from an early years setting to school, or from primary to secondary school, with an existing history of requiring SEN provision.

For many children, however, special educational needs are identified in the course of a key stage, usually as a result of expressions of concern by teachers or parents/carers. Personalisation, however, offers a more systematic route to identifying children who may require extra help in one form or another. It requires that class or subject teachers track all pupils' progress using ongoing assessment supplemented by discrete assessment tasks and tests, and review each child's progress regularly.

These reviews, held two to three times a year, should consider data on prior and current attainment, attendance and behaviour, and identify any pupil who is not on track to achieve the levels of attainment for which they are targeted. In a primary school, this review might be the trigger for the class teacher to discuss what extra steps could be taken to accelerate the child's progress with the INCO, SENCO, ethnic minority achievement (EMA) coordinator, G & T coordinator or the person who leads on behaviour. In the secondary school, the information on pupils who are struggling is expected to be fed to the year leader, whose role it is identify pupils causing concern in a number of subjects because of effort/behaviour, academic progress or attendance. The year leader in turn works with other middle managers to determine which interventions might be needed to support the pupil – some of which might come under the aegis of the SENCO/INCO.

Much guidance is available to support class and subject teachers in how to track and assess pupil attainment levels, so as to identify pupils who are experiencing difficulties. *Tracking for success* (DfES, 2005g) suggests that teachers assess against those learning objectives that are key indicators of pupils' progress, focusing particularly on those that can be related to crucial level borderlines between NC levels, for example between Level 3 and 4 in the primary school and Level 4 and 5 in the secondary school.

The SENCO's or INCO's role can usefully be to 'coach' subject teachers and class teachers in upper Key Stage 2, so that they are able to assess against NC levels and sub-levels at which pupils with SEN or disabilities may be working. Teachers will need help in recognising, for example, the key indicators of progress from Level 1 to Level 2, and Level 2 to Level 3, as well as those from Level 3 upwards. In time, subject teachers and primary teachers might also be expected to develop skills in assessing against the 'P' levels, with the help of the SENCO.

SENCOs/INCOs can also support colleagues' assessment skills by providing training, modelling and coaching on child–adult conferences, aimed at obtaining 'a window into the child's mind' and acquiring a deeper and shared understanding of what it is that holds the pupil back and what can help them as a learner. Such conferences, in the form of 'learning conversations', are suggested in National Strategies' guidance and by the Gilbert Review in the form of meetings with the 'learning guide'.

Children with the more severe learning difficulties and with the behaviour difficulties we might class as SEN, however, will need more in-depth assessment. SENCOs/INCOs have a crucial role in contributing specialist expertise to assessment that seeks to establish not only that a given pupil is not trying hard, behaving well or making progress, but also *why*. Such an assessment might involve one or more of the following: classroom observation, use of questionnaires, standardised tests, analysis of children's work, analysis of underlying perceptual, motor or memory skills, or gathering information from parents/carers. A range of tools a SENCO/INCO can use are suggested in *Special educational needs in the primary school* (Gross, 2002). An hour spent on this kind of assessment and feeding the outcomes into the kinds of child profiles we met in Chapter 2 will make more difference than many hours spent organising IEPs.

The importance of this kind of assessment is to identify the child's strengths, so that they can be helped to draw on them, and barriers to learning, so that plans can be made to overcome them. It is a moot point whether assessment also needs to attach a diagnostic label to the child or not. In some cases, formally identifying individuals and making special plans for them appears to hinder their progress rather than help. For example, in Chapter 1 we saw how pupils identified as having ADHD made less progress than similar pupils whose teachers were simply given information sheets about general strategies for inattentive and overactive pupils. Similarly, recent research has shown (Freeman, 2001) that children labelled as gifted were far more likely to experience emotional and social difficulties at school and in later life than were those with equally high IQs who were not labelled. But on the other hand, there is evidence that some labels, such as dyslexia and Asperger's syndrome (Gross, 1994; Papps and Dyson, 2004) are actively helpful because they help adults to respond in more effective ways to behaviours that they might otherwise construe as evidence of 'laziness', 'bad behaviour' and so on.

Failure to make appropriate adaptations to learning and teaching is a risk if particular impairments or disabilities are missed because the school lacks effective procedures to identify them. Tales of pupils subsequently discovered to have serious hearing loss or visual impairment after years of failure are not apocryphal. For this reason, effective SENCOs/INCOs build periodic screening into the school's tracking systems, with staff using quick checklists during meetings to pick up pupils with minor hearing loss or visual impairment, language difficulties, dyslexia, motor difficulties or problems relating to their emotional health and well-being (Gross, 2002).

In these ways the SENCO's or INCO's expertise can serve to enhance the school's current system for identifying pupils who need additional support. The principle, however, is of **building on** the system, rather than creating a new one. And it is the trend towards increasing personalisation that makes this possible.

5 | Setting Targets and Monitoring Progress

Setting targets

Setting targets for pupils with SEN is a non-negotiable. In order to comply with the SEN Code of Practice (2001b) schools must:

- identify learning targets for individual pupils with SEN;
- plan provision that is additional to or different from the differentiated curriculum offered to all pupils;
- review provision in the light of individual pupil outcomes.

Chapter 7 of this book will examine ways of planning and reviewing additional provision, other than through IEPs. In this chapter we will look at how target setting (and even more important, target getting) can be embedded within whole-school systems rather than make extra work for SENCOs/INCOs and teachers.

The current context of personalised target setting and record keeping promotes such embedding. The process starts with setting individual progress targets that say what NC level or sub-level the pupil is aiming to achieve at the end of the key stage and – working backwards from that – the end of each year. These are *numerical* targets. They are not the same as the kinds of targets we see on IEPs, but they fulfil a function that is missing in an IEP-driven system. In such a system small-steps targets are set for what the pupil will know, understand and be able to do at the end of each term or six-month review period. But no longer-term goals are set, and it is possible for the pupil to achieve all the IEP targets but not make the 'level jumps' in attainment that are possible and achieved by other pupils with similar learning needs.

The point about numerical targets is that they are based on data, such as that provided by the Fischer Family Trust. Using RAISEonline or similar local systems, they benchmark the pupil against others with similar starting points and predict what they ought to be able to achieve. The comparisons with national progress rates – for example, an expectation that Year 7 pupils should achieve two sub-levels' progress in the year – inject challenge into an SEN system that can easily become cosy and complacent.

These comparisons with national progress rates are not yet perfect. We know what the chances are of a pupil at a given starting point achieving a particular end of key stage level, but not yet what the chances are of a pupil at a given starting point who also has special needs in communication and interaction achieving a particular end of key stage level, or a pupil with BESD, or difficulties in cognition and learning, or a physical impairment, or any combination of these. The national data have not yet been refined to take in SEN types. Nor, at the moment, do they include information to help schools set numerical targets for pupils functioning at 'P' scales levels – though in time, these will come, and many local authorities already furnish schools with information of this kind. But they do provide a good starting point, that can be moderated using teacher professional knowledge about the child and what is available within the school or setting (including intervention programmes) to accelerate progress and 'add value' to the predicted levels of attainment.

Numerical targets for pupils with SEN or a disability are, moreover, very motivating for the individual. To know which level you are at and which level you are aiming for is immensely helpful, if combined with knowledge of what it is you need to do in order to reach that level. And that is the essential next step – turning the numerical target into *curricular* targets.

Curricular targets, phrased in 'I can…' terms, describe what it is the pupil has to learn in order to make the necessary learning jumps that will keep them on track to reach their numerical targets. The process of arriving at them is described in a number of government publications – the planning unit in *Excellence and enjoyment: learning and teaching in the primary years* (DfES, 2004b) and the *Assessment for learning* secondary materials (DfES, 2004a).

The *Tracking for success* materials (DfES, 2005g) supply a helpful definition: 'Curricular targets are the link between pupils' long term numerical targets and the next steps in their learning, described in lesson learning objectives.' They define *key* pieces of learning that children will work on over about half a term; they are broader than lesson objectives, which are often specific to the particular content of a given lesson. They often stem from a whole-school target.

For example (Figure 5.1), a secondary school might analyse its pupils' results and decide that a priority is to improve enquiry skills in science. This whole-school curricular target is then 'layered' into age-related targets so that each year group has its own curricular targets. In Year 7 the target might be 'Pupils can plan their own investigation.' This is then layered further into medium-term curricular targets for each half term or unit of work. *Tracking for success* gives the example 'In an investigation pupils are able to identify the key variables that they can and cannot control.' In pupil-speak, this becomes a group or pupil target 'I will focus on planning my own investigation, say what I think will happen, what will change and what I will measure.'

How might this be relevant to a pupil with SEN or a disability? If the pupil has difficulties in cognition and learning, the target might be differentiated so as to focus on the skill of prediction (a valuable, cross-curricular learning-to-learn skill that the teacher knows will be relevant to the pupil's progress in a wide range of social and learning situations). Over a series of lessons the pupil's target might then be 'I will tell my teacher or a friend what I think what will happen in our investigation.'

In English (Figure 5.2), a Key Stage 3 target to ensure that pupils use paragraphs appropriately might 'layer' back to a Year 8 target, 'When writing, pupils use topic sentences to begin paragraphs', and a group target 'I can write a paragraph using a topic sentence, and group points so that they are clear and support the topic sentence.' For a pupil with learning difficulties, the *individual* target might be 'I can plan clear sections for my writing' (a target taken from the core learning in Year 2 in text organisation and structure in the Primary Literacy renewed Framework).

FIGURE 5.1 Layered curricular target for science

FIGURE 5.2 Layered curricular target for English

In the primary school, Primary Strategy guidance (DfES, 2004f) suggests three levels of differentiated curricular targets in any given class – targets for pupils performing above age-related expectations, targets for pupils performing at age-related expectations, and targets for pupils performing below age-related expectations. The guidance also emphasises, however, that some children will require a further level of personalisation, with individual targets set where appropriate.

As an example (Figure 5.3), when working on measurement for length the overall curricular target for a Year 2 class might be 'To estimate, measure and compare lengths using standard units.' For an average group, the differentiated target might be 'I can estimate the lengths of different objects, compare their size and measure them and compare their length', for the more able 'I can measure a length in centimetres, find half and double the length in centimetres and millimetres', for a lower-attaining group 'I can measure and compare the length of different objects using ruler lengths.' For a child with SEN the personalised target might be 'I can compare the lengths of two ribbons or necklaces.'

Good sources of curricular targets in core subjects are the core learning in literacy and mathematics by strand in the renewed Primary Frameworks, and for secondary the Progression Maps that allow teachers to identify descriptors that fit particular groups of pupils or individuals, and then suggest relevant next-step core targets. For example, in English the Progression Maps for reading suggest the characteristics of the 'developing

Year 2 curricular target:
To estimate, measure and compare lengths using standard units.

Above average group:
I can measure a length in centimetres, find half and double the length in centimetres and millimetres.

Average group:
I can estimate the length of different objects, compare their size and measure them and compare their length.

Lower-attaining group:
I can measure and compare the length of different objects using ruler lengths.

Child with SEN:
I can compare the lengths of two ribbons or necklaces.

FIGURE 5.3 Layered curricular target for measurement

reader' (below Level 3), the 'secure developing reader' (Level 3), the 'competent reader' (Level 4), the 'active reader' (Level 5), the 'reflective reader' (Level 6) and the 'versatile reader' (above Level 6). Examples of pupil work are given for each of these. If the teacher thinks that the description 'sounds like my pupils' they can then click on a menu for a list of relevant next-step curricular targets, and ideas on how to help a pupil achieve them.

In the Progression Maps for mathematics, each strand of learning is broken down into curricular targets appropriate at different ability levels. Handling data, for example, shows the progression from Step 1 (NC Level 2), 'Solve a given problem by organising and interpreting numerical data in simple lists, tables and graphs' through to Step 10 'Identify possible sources of bias and plan how to minimise it' (Year 9).

Curricular targets need not be confined to the core subjects. They can also embrace social and emotional learning. For example (Figure 5.4), a school might decide on a whole-school target that children will work well together in groups. Using the social and emotional aspects of learning (SEAL) materials (DfES, 2005a) they might then set layered targets for each year group. In Year 6 the target might be 'When working in a group I can tell others if I agree/don't agree with them and why, and listen to others' views, thinking about what they have said.' But some children might not yet have secured earlier learning and have a personal target taken from Year R, 'I can take turns in a group.'

FIGURE 5.4 Layered curricular target for social and emotional learning

Setting differentiated curricular targets for pupils with additional needs has the great advantage of keeping the targets within the realm of the class or subject teacher. The targets are linked closely to the work of the class as a whole and will be addressed through the teacher's regular differentiated classroom planning. They have a much better chance, therefore, of guiding teaching and learning than the computer-generated, filing-cabinet targets that characterise too many IEPs.

The SEAL progression in both primary and secondary materials, the facility in the renewed Primary Literacy and Mathematics Frameworks for teachers to track back to find linked but earlier core learning objectives, and the exceptionally helpful secondary Progression Maps tool all also mean that class and subject teachers *should* now be expected to set differentiated curricular targets for all their pupils, including those who are performing well below age-related expectations. This is the key to a reduction in the SENCO's/INCO's workload. It is also the key to better progress for children who experience barriers to their learning.

Differentiated curricular targets set by the class or subject teacher also have disadvantages, however. While they may be highly relevant to the direction the whole school, class or group is taking, they may not be particularly relevant to the unique and pressing needs of the pupil with SEN or a disability. IEP targets, when arrived at through a shared, group process of prioritising problems (as described in Chapter 1), do help everyone to focus on what really matters. And what really matters is likely to be:

- a problem which the child feels is important and on which they want to work – that is, one which ties in with their main life concerns at the time (like 'learn to do joined-up writing' when the child is really bothered by the difference they have just begun to notice between their written work and that of their peers);
- a problem which underpins others – such as poor concentration, personal organisation or willingness to tackle something new.

Such priorities are often cross-curricular, may relate to the five ECM outcomes, and will not be addressed solely by curricular targets set by subject teachers, or literacy and mathematics targets set by primary teachers.

Cross-curricular, highly personal targets are not unique to children with SEN or disabilities, however. All children have particular things they want and need to improve on or achieve that are about themselves as individuals rather than as subject-fodder. And as we saw in Chapter 2, some schools do expect all children to set themselves a personal target of high relevance to their immediate concerns. The role of the SENCO/INCO may be to ensure that whole-school target-setting systems do include this element. SENCOs/INCOs are likely to have considerable expertise in devising such targets, and in making them specific, measurable, achievable and time-constrained ('SMART'). They might engage this expertise to provide pupils, form tutors and class teachers with banks of example targets on which they can draw, covering behaviour, study, organisational, 'learning to learn' and life skills. This would be a very good application for the IEP software that many schools have bought, which often has excellent target banks.

Whole-school systems for setting and reviewing personal targets, as distinct from simply subject targets, are encouraged by the Secondary National Strategy in their suggested 'learning conversations', where pupils talk about their overall progress as a learner. The Gilbert Review suggests that these conversations are undertaken by a 'learning guide'. Such discussions should focus on the pupil's overall learning needs, and consider progress not only in subject learning but also in so-called soft or non-cognitive skills such as communication, the ability to work as part of a team, reliability, punctuality and perseverance, knowing how to work independently without close supervision, and remaining resilient in the face of difficulties.

If whole-school systems for setting personal targets that transcend subject boundaries are not in place, however, a system for pupils with SEN or disabilities might be the one in operation at Coombe Boys' in the case study in Chapter 2. Here, teaching assistants join in the academic mentoring days and contribute suggestions for appropriate personal, cross-curricular targets to the meeting between form tutor and pupil.

Tracking progress

Tracking overall curricular progress

As with target setting, systems for tracking the progress of *all* pupils on the curricular and numerical targets set with and for them are now expected of all schools. Ofsted (2006b), for example, identifies 'Rigorous tracking of personal development and academic progress of individuals, particular groups and cohorts of pupils as a key feature of effective schools.'

The most effective tracking systems for pupils with SEN or disabilities will be embedded within the systems already maintained for the class or group. This ensures that class or subject teachers are monitoring their pupils' progress throughout the year and have ownership and responsibility for taking action where any pupil's progress is causing concern. The SENCO's/INCO's role will be to develop and refine whole-school tracking systems so that they are fully inclusive and so that all pupils' progress is systematically monitored and reviewed, with the findings acted on.

Tables 5.1 and 5.2 show examples of tracking systems typically operated in primary schools, developed in the Intensifying Support Programme (DfES, 2006f) and adapted here to include pupils with learning difficulties. Children's names are entered each term against the NC level they have reached. The shaded areas show the NC levels that correspond to nationally expected attainment. The tracking sheet shows at a glance those pupils who are not moving at the rate they should be over the course of the year.

Use of such systems is made easier where the school maintains assessment systems that automatically link the child's everyday learning to NC sub-levels. A school employing the Ruth Miskin literacy programme, for example, can link the level of story-books children are reading to an NC sub-level (Table 5.3). A school applying Reading Recovery principles to run daily guided reading groups in Year 1 and 2 can similarly use the Reading Recovery book levels to track progress against the National Curriculum (Table 5.4).

	Summer Year 1	Autumn Year 2	Spring Year 2	Summer Year 2
Upper L3/3a				Simrun
Secure L3/3b		Simrun	Simrun	Mehnaz Marion
Lower L3/3c	Simrun			Mahfuza
Upper L2/2a		Mehnaz Marion	Mahfuza Sofia Mehnaz Marion	Anass Ruby Chloe Charlotte Sofia
Secure L2/2b	Mehnaz Marion	Anass Mahfuza	Anass Ruby Chloe Charlotte	Sumayyah Shaylayne Michal Jennifer Rhiannon Georgia Ioana Anthony Jem Mikaeel
Lower L2/2c	Mahfuza	Ruby Chloe Charlotte Sofia	Joshua Sumayyah Shaylayne Michal Jennifer Rhiannon Georgia Ioana Anthony Jem Mikaeel	Joshua Erin Jacob Caitlin
Upper L1/1a	Ruby Chloe Charlotte Sofia	Sumayyah Shaylayne Michal Jennifer Rhiannon Georgia Ioana Anthony Jem Mikaeel	Erin Jacob Caitlin	Finlay Lemin Joseph
Secure L1/1b	Erin Sumayyah Shaylayne Michal Jennifer Rhiannon Georgia Ioana Anthony Jem Mikaeel	Joshua Erin Jacob Caitlin	Finlay Lemin Joseph	Tia Aiisha Meia
Lower L1/1c	Lemin Joshua Jacob Caitlin	Shivan Tia Aiisha Meia Finlay Lemin Joseph	Shivan Tia Aiisha Meia	Shivan Kitty
W/1c	Kitty Shivan Tia Aiisha Meia Finlay Joseph	Kitty	Nermien Kitty	Nermien
P4/5/6	Nermien	Nermien		

TABLE 5.1 Tracking progress: Year 2 Reading

Upper L4/4a			
Secure L4/4b			
Lower L4/4c			Mary Ann
Upper L3/3a		Mary Ann	Mary Ann	Zakiriya
Secure L3/3b	Mary Ann	Ronan	Ronan Zakiriya Marsha	Marsha Grace Aysa
Lower L3/3c		Ronan	Grace Aysa	Jasmine Destiney Lily Eren Samir Joshua
Upper L2/2a	Ronan Zakiriya	Zakiriya Marsha Grace Joshua Aysa	Jasmine Destiney Lily Eren Samir Joshua	Julia Dea Rocco Helen Suruti Jordis Gulse
Secure L2/2b	Marsha Grace Aysa	Jasmine Lily Eren Samir	Julia Dea Rocco Helen Suruti Jordis Gulse	Jumana Yasir Pia Siddita Holly
Lower L2/2c	Jasmine Destiney Lily Eren Samir Joshua	Julia Destiney Dea Rocco Helen Suruti Jordis	Jumana Yasir Pia Siddita Holly	Daniel Josphine
Upper L1/1a	Julia Dea Rocco Helen Suruti Jordis Gulse	Yasir Pia Siddita Holly Gulse	Daniel Josphine	
Secure L1/1b	Jumana Yasir Pia Siddita Holly	Jumana Daniel Josphine	Patrick Melissa	Patrick Katie Melissa
Lower L1/1c	Daniel Josphine		Melissa	Katie
W/1c	Patrick Katie Melissa	Patrick Katie		Alfie
P4/5/6	Alfie	Alfie	Alfie	
	Summer Year 2	**Autumn Year 3**	**Spring Year 3**	**Summer Year 3**

TABLE 5.2 Tracking progress: Year 3 Mathematics

CLASS: Sticklebacks Class Tracking Sheet for RML	SCHOOL YEAR: 2006 Year – 06/07			
	Reception Summer 06	Year 1 Autumn 06	Spring 07	Summer 07
Passage 6 Unlikely that child needs RML.				
Set 7 story books. Level 2b/A. Revise set 2. Teach set 3.				
Passage 5. Level 2c/b Sets 6 story books. Teach set 2 and 3 speed sounds.				
Passage 4 Level 2c Set 5 story books. Teach set 2 and 3 speed sounds.				
Set 4 Story books. Level 1b/A Revise set 2 speed sounds. Teach set 3 speed sounds.				
Passage 2 Level 1c/b Sets 3 story books. Teach set 2 speed sounds. Practise set 1. Pronunciation.				
Set 2 story books. Level 1c Teach set 2 speed sounds.		Clare James Isabella Henry Sophie Sian Kai		
Passage 2 Level W/1c Set 1 story books. Teach set 2 speed sounds. Practise set 1. Pronunciation.	Clare James Isabella Henry Sophie Sian	Duncan Anna Mia Katie Jeremy Matthew Lucy		
Passage 1. The ditties. Level W Practise set 1 with pure pronunciation.	Duncan Anna Mia Katie Jeremy Matthew Lucy	Jason George Hannah Emily Charlotte Amy		
No passage many sounds. Teach set 1 speed sounds. Child can blend using Fred talk.	Jason George Hannah Emily Charlotte Amy Kai	Mary Julia Fiona Molly Ben		
No passage, few sounds. Teach all set 1 speed sounds. Teach Fred talk.	Carla Ben Mary Rachel Hannah Julia	Carla		

TABLE 5.3 Tracking using Ruth Miskin literacy book levels

PUPIL NAME	SEPTEMBER 2005		JANUARY 2006		JULY 2006	
	RR book level	NC level	RR book level	NC level	RR book level	NC level
Amy	1	W				
Katherine	1	W				
Peaches	1	W				
Mohammed	1	W				
Sean	1	W				
Ibrahim	1	W				
Fatima	1	W				
Jasmin	1	W				
Olivia	1	W				
Grace	1	W				
Jack	1	W				
Cameron	1	W				
Jamie	2	W				
Megan	2	W				
Erin	2	W				
Kyle	2	W				
Harry	2	W				
Charlie	2	W				
Iqra	2	W				
Abdul	2	W				
Ruby	2	W				
Sophie	3	W				
Hamza	3	W				
William	5	1C				
Thomas	5	1C				
Lily L	5	1C				
Oliver	5	1C				
Morgan	5	1C				
Cameron	11	1B				
Callum	19	2C				
Lily B	22	2B				

TABLE 5.4 Tracking NC progress using Reading Recovery book levels

Tracking systems like these are helpful in setting high expectations, enabling class teachers to identify all pupils not on track to achieve nationally expected levels. They can then seek advice from the SENCO or other inclusion specialists (such as EMA coordinator or lead teacher for intervention) on appropriate interventions to enable these children to catch up.

They do, however, run the risk of leaving out that very small group of pupils for whom achieving national benchmark levels is not an appropriate expectation. For this reason, a more inclusive tracking system will gather termly information on whether each child is on track to meet their own individual numerical targets. At Kentish Town Primary School in London, for example, each class teacher receives a termly printout showing which children have exceeded, which have met and which have fallen short of their termly NC sub-level targets. A simple traffic-light system (green for progress ahead of expected progress towards end of year targets, amber for on target and red for below expected progress) is also used in some schools. The SENCO's/INCO's role is then to monitor the proportion of pupils with SEN or disabilities (or, if they are inclusion coordinator, pupils from other vulnerable groups such as EAL learners or Gifted and Talented pupils) who are on amber or green.

In the secondary phase, the system used at Coombe Boys' School in Kingston fulfils a similar purpose. Each pupil's end-of-term 'Position Statement' tells them whether they are on track to achieve their numerical targets.

Effective schools will also keep track of pupils' year-on-year progress. If this is not part of whole-school systems, the SENCO/INCO can keep such individual records for pupils with SEN, adding information on additional provision that was in place in a given year or term (Tables 5.5 and 5.6). Nothing will impress an Ofsted inspector more than this kind of overview.

Child X		MATHS	SPEAKING AND LISTENING	READING	WRITING
November '05 **Support:** **Social skills: 2 × 20 min per week**		P5	P5	P5	P5
March '06 **LSA 1:1 in class 10 min/day** **Sp&lang group of 2, 3 × 20 min/week** **Lit group every day** **Reading group 2 × week**		P6	P5	P4	P6
November '06 *Place to be* **provision** **Plus the above support continued**		P8	P7	P8	P6
Update January 2007: CAMHS referral made. All support continues. Most ability levels have remained the same.					

d.o.b. 03.04.00

TABLE 5.5 Overview of support and progress

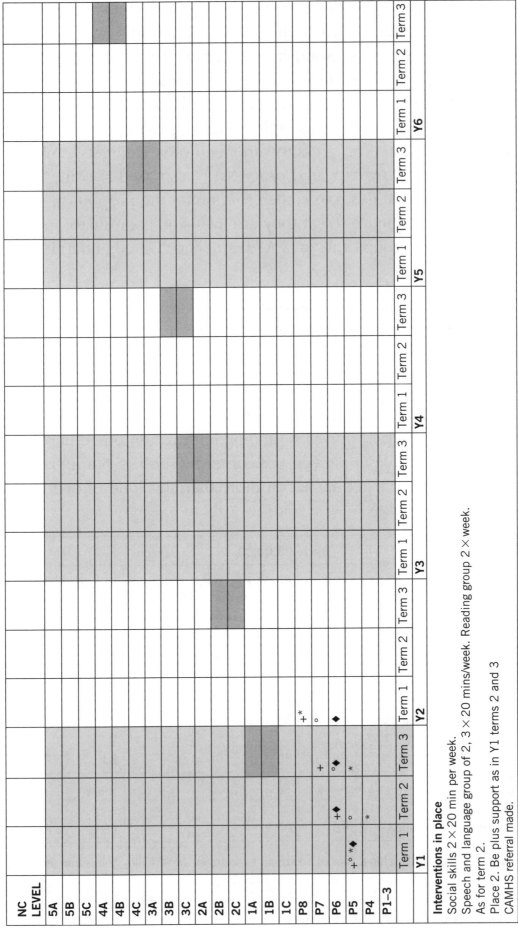

Interventions in place
Social skills 2 × 20 min per week.
Speech and language group of 2, 3 × 20 mins/week. Reading group 2 × week.
As for term 2.
Place 2. Be plus support as in Y1 terms 2 and 3
CAMHS referral made.

Expected English and Maths level for age group shaded
* Child's reading level ◆ Writing level + maths level ° Speaking and listening level

TABLE 5.6 Example of a cumulative tracking sheet for a Year 2 child

Tracking like this needs to be informed by a secure knowledge of what constitutes satisfactory progress – approximately three NC level 'points' over a school year in Key Stages 2 and 3, using the points system shown in Table 5.7 below.

Reliable information on what constitutes satisfactory progress for pupils working at the level of the 'P' scales will not be available from the DfES via RAISEonline until there is sufficient 'P' scale data collected nationally, probably some years after it becomes mandatory in the summer of 2008. Local authorities, however, may have access to previous data collected at Durham University and may be able to suggest appropriate benchmarks.

Progress over the course of an intervention

A second element of tracking that is specific to pupils with additional needs is tracking progress over the course of an intervention, using 'before' and 'after' measures. A small-group intervention to improve pupils' social, emotional and

NC LEVEL	SUB-LEVEL	POINTS
P3		1
P4		1.5
P5		2
P6		2.5
P7		3
P8		5
1	1c 1b 1a	7 9 11
2	2c 2b 2a	13 15 17
3	3c 3b 3a	19 21 23
4	4c 4b 4a	25 27 29
5	5c 5b 5a	31 33 35
6	6c 6b 6a	37 39 41
7	7c 7b 7a	43 45 47

TABLE 5.7 The National Curriculum points system

behavioural skills might, for example, feature a before and after assessment using NFER Nelson's emotional literacy measures, or the Goodman Strengths and Difficulties Questionnaire. Children in a nurture group would be assessed at the beginning and end of their placement with the aid of the Boxall Profile. Children taking part in a literacy intervention might have their reading or spelling age assessed via one of a number of standardised tests. Suggestions for appropriate measures can be found in *Leading on intervention* (DfES, 2006d). A useful proforma for collecting pre-and post-intervention data can be found in the toolkit section of this book.

Evaluation

All these tracking systems have the added advantage of making possible something that IEPs can never achieve – allowing the SENCO/INCO or senior management team (SMT) to evaluate the effectiveness of particular interventions, and the progress of pupils with SEN or disabilities in their school. They can, for example, answer the questions:

- What percentage of lower-attaining pupils and those with SEN or disabilities met their end of year or key stage numerical targets, and how does this compare with the percentage of pupils without SEN or disabilities achieving their targets?
- Which interventions are proving effective in helping pupils with SEN or disabilities meet their numerical targets? Which aren't?
- Does RAISEonline show that the value added progress of pupils with SEN or disabilities in our school is at least as good as the national progress?
- Have we increased the percentage of pupils with SEN or disabilities meeting their numerical targets since last year, and what did we do to achieve this?

Reviewing progress

Just as the SEN Code of Practice requires that schools track pupil progress made as a result of additional or different provision, so it also requires a regular and frequent review schedule for individuals.

This need not mean a lot of extra work or separate SEN procedures. Our case study schools in Chapter 2 were all successful in combining the review requirements of the Code with what they did for all pupils – twice-yearly parent meetings extended from ten to 30 minutes for children with SEN, or academic mentoring days at which TAs join pupils, tutor and perhaps head of year to take stock of progress.

Again, these integrated systems have the advantage of keeping ownership of the progress of pupils with SEN or disabilities where it belongs – with those who are immediately responsible for their subject learning and pastoral care.

Refinements for pupils with SEN or disabilities will, however, be necessary. Reviews must, for example, look at progress across the curriculum and often behavioural, organisational, study, life and 'learning-to-learn' skills as well as progress in individual subjects. This is particularly important in secondary schools where uneven performance across subjects can often give vital clues about what helps and what hinders a pupil's learning or behaviour. The reviews must be one to one, unlike the group 'learning conversations' between class teacher or form tutor and target pupils advocated by the National Strategies.

Review systems for pupils with SEN or disabilities should also build in a review of the extent to which pupils' classroom curricular and personal targets have been met, as well as overall numerical progress in NC levels, sub-levels and 'P' scales.

They should review not only the pupil's progress but also the effectiveness of the school's actions. Is there evidence from teachers' differentiated planning, for example, that staff are taking account of the pupil's individual needs? Have any additional interventions undertaken proved effective, on the evidence from before and after measures and evidence from what the pupil, parents/carers and staff all think? Is further intervention necessary, and if so which types of support from the school's provision map might be appropriate?

These review questions help hold the school to account for what it is doing to support the pupil. Review meetings also represent an opportunity to hold everyone involved (pupil, parents/carers, staff, outside agencies) to account for any actions they agreed to undertake at the last meeting or review.

Another added dimension to review meetings that involve pupils with SEN or disabilities is the cast list involved. While reviews for most students may only involve pupil, parent/carer and class teacher or form tutor, those for pupils with SEN or disabilities might also involve the SENCO/INCO, perhaps the head of year in a secondary school, and any outside agencies that are involved.

Finally, additional work may need to be done with both pupils and parents/carers to secure their confident engagement in review meetings. This is discussed in Chapter 8.

The additional elements in SEN reviews mean that the SENCO/INCO may want to build on regular school record keeping by adding extra headings or prompts. A possible set of agenda prompts is included in the toolkit section of this book.

Summary

This chapter has considered ways in which practices suggested by the SEN Code can increasingly be subsumed within whole-school systems for setting targets for pupils and tracking their subsequent progress.

It has also suggested extra features that might need to be added to whole-school systems, if they are to fully meet the very particular needs of pupils who in some way fall outside the norm. These additional features are summarised in Table 5.8 below.

WHOLE-SCHOOL SYSTEMS	SEN ADAPTATIONS
Target setting – numerical	Use RAISEonline and local authority data to set numerical targets for pupils functioning well below age-related expectations, including those working at 'P' levels.
Target setting – curricular	Teach class and subject teachers how to track back to identify curricular targets for pupils functioning well below age-related expectations, including those working at 'P' levels.
	Provide banks of targets for behaviour, study, organisational, 'learning-to-learn' and life skills.
Tracking progress	Monitor the impact of intervention programmes by using 'before' and 'after' data.
	Monitor the progress of pupils with SEN and disabilities towards numerical targets, as a group.
Reviewing progress	Ensure that reviews
	• are cross-curricular;
	• include a review of the achievement of curricular and personal targets;
	• are individual, rather than involving a group;
	• involve others beyond the pupil, tutor or class teacher and parent – for example, SENCO, head of year, TA/key worker, outside agencies;
	• consider how effective the school's provision has proved to be;
	• check whether all concerned have completed the actions they undertook to take at the last meeting or review;
	• are preceded by work to secure the confident participation of pupil and parents/carers.

TABLE 5.8 Suggested adaptations to existing systems

Achieving Targets
Adaptations to Everyday Classroom Teaching

Three things make a real difference to the achievement of children with SEN or disabilities. They are:

1 Additional provision made by the school, in the form of time-limited, evidence-based intervention programmes to address gaps in children's language, literacy, mathematical and social and emotional learning.
2 Interventions that extend beyond the school and involve outside agencies, from disabled children's services to youth offending teams, in providing support to the child in the context of the family and community.
3 Adaptations to everyday classroom teaching, signalled via teachers' medium- and short-term planning.

This chapter is about the last of these three. It is about whole-school systems that expect all teachers to take account of the needs of pupils with SEN or disabilities (and for that matter more able pupils, EAL learners and other vulnerable groups) when they plan their teaching, and monitor whether this expectation is being met.

Successfully embedding thinking about SEN and disabilities into teachers' planning is essential to beating bureaucracy (see Figure 6.1). Like setting targets and tracking progress for all pupils, it enables schools to use everyday systems that already exist in order to cater for SEN, rather than separate paper trails.

IEPs were intended to be the mechanism for influencing teachers' planning. But, as we saw in the case studies in Chapter 2, there is little evidence that they have successfully done so. On the other hand, the case studies show that class and subject teachers do appear to make use of pupil profiles provided by the SENCO, when combined with planning formats which have an extra column, row or cell in which teachers are expected to record the differentiation that will be in place for pupils with SEN.

Embedding SEN and disability in teachers' planning takes time and effort,

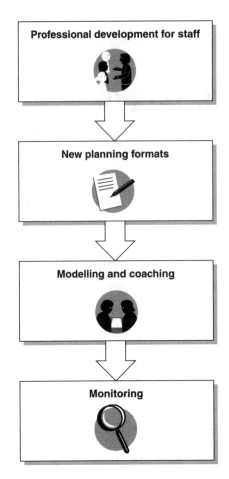

FIGURE 6.1 A four-part strategy to embed thinking about SEN

however. First, there will need to be professional development for all staff on the basic principles. Second, it may be necessary to introduce new planning formats, or amend existing ones. Third, SENCOs/INCOs need to spend time working alongside class and subject teachers to model and coach the process of differentiated planning. Fourth, the school will need to consider building the requirement to plan for pupils with additional needs into performance management. They will also need to build in systems for monitoring teachers' planning to identify staff who may need further support or challenge.

Mapping out this four-part strategy can take care of another potential piece of bureaucracy – the requirement to produce a plan showing how curriculum access will be ensured for disabled pupils. The SENCO/INCO can simply identify the actions that need to be taken (staff training, modelling/coaching, adapting planning formats and performance management) into the school improvement or development plan. Recent government guidance makes it clear (IRU, 2007) that embedding curriculum access plans into overall school development plans is an acceptable and sensible step.

Professional development for staff

The National Curriculum (QCA, 2000) statutory inclusion statement sets out three key principles essential to planning and teaching:

1 setting suitable learning challenges;
2 responding to pupils' diverse learning needs;
3 overcoming potential barriers to learning and assessment for individuals and groups of pupils.

These principles form the basis for professional development that SENCOs/INCOs can offer staff. The National Strategies suggest a way of translating the principles into practice, and a way of presenting them visually (Figure 6.2).

 Learning objectives

SENCOs/INCOs can explain to staff that, when planning for a class, they need first to think about the range of learning objectives that they aim to cover. The majority of the class will be working on an objective linked to age-related expectations. Some pupils, however, will need to work on objectives that are more advanced, others on objectives that come earlier in the progression set out in the relevant curriculum frameworks or programmes of study. This will apply even in setted classes. In many

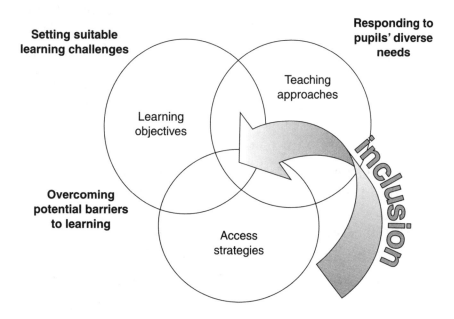

FIGURE 6.2 The circles of inclusion

schools, the range can be very great – from P3 to Level 4a in maths in one Year 3 class, for example.

Teachers plan for this range of ability in different ways. Typically, they may plan activities at three levels – for a group of pupils working below age-related expectations, a group at age-related expectations, and a group who should be expected to achieve above age-related expectations.

For some children with SEN or disabilities, and pupils who are highly gifted, there is a need for a further level of planning, often at an individual level. This should describe arrangements for those who are working well below, or well above, age-related expectations.

It is this level of planning that is often missed out, generally because teachers are uncertain about learning objectives that lie outside the usual terrain, and have not had the opportunity to work alongside an expert in planning how to help pupils achieve them. They tend to plan (Ofsted, 2004) 'how pupils with SEN could be engaged rather than on what pupils needed to learn next … this was a common reason why a significant number of pupils with SEN made too little progress'.

There is a problem, too, in the planning that many teachers do at even the three levels of below, at and above age-related expectations – the 'must/should/could' that we could call 'normal differentiation'. All too often the differentiation is based on outcomes rather than learning objectives. The group working at below-average expectations is simply expected to produce less in terms of outcomes (a sentence instead of a paragraph, for example), while the learning objective remains the same for the whole class. Alternatively, the planning simply notes that the lower-attaining group will be supported by a TA to achieve the general class learning objective (or at least remain reasonably quiet while everyone else does).

What SENCOs/INCOs will want to encourage colleagues to do is write into their planning *different* learning objectives for groups and in some cases individuals, all linked into the same overall class focus.

The revised National Strategies Literacy and Numeracy Frameworks for the Primary Phase, and the Secondary Progression Maps, model the way in which a teacher can take a learning objective for a particular group and track forwards (for more able pupils) and backwards (for lower-attaining) to find linked objectives appropriate to the needs of individuals or groups. The structure and the electronic format of the revised Primary Frameworks support such multi-level curriculum planning, and allow teachers to easily track back through a progression strand to locate earlier, and later, learning objectives. The interactivity offered by the electronic framework enables exemplar teaching units to be amended so that teachers can add in differentiated learning objectives.

The principle of identifying different learning objectives for individuals and groups is one that staff easily grasp. Equally, the teachers will understand that planning differentiated learning objectives will give a focus to the work of additional adults providing support in the classroom. Research (Moyles and Suschitzky, 1997) has shown that teaching assistants tend to focus more on helping children complete tasks successfully (what children are meant to *do*) rather than on what they are meant to *learn*. Differentiated learning objectives that are communicated to TAs can stop this happening.

Even though they see the advantages and support the principle, the idea of multiple learning objectives can still nevertheless sometimes alarm staff. How, they will ask, are they expected to teach a class of 30 children working on a number of different learning objectives?

There is no point in pretending that this is easy; better to say that it represents the peak of a teacher's skilled performance, something to work towards and something that even the most skilled teacher will not achieve all of the time. Even so, people will be able to give you examples of how, when they are in the 'exposition' phase of the lesson, they are able to drop in questions at different levels, targeted at different named pupils, or reiterate an explanation of a concept covered last year for the benefit of pupils who are still trying to master that particular idea.

They will even be more easily able to give examples of how they design tasks at different levels for the part of the lesson when pupils are working independently or in groups – this is part of every teacher's planning repertoire. Practical help, too, is increasingly available through the National Strategies. The planning sections of the revised Primary Literacy and Mathematics Frameworks, for example, have direct links to resources for pupils working above, below or well below age-related expectations for any given unit of work. Table 6.1 gives an example.

In training colleagues, SENCOs/INCOs will want to help them consider the assessment for learning guidance in the Table 6.1 example. The plenary part

CHILDREN'S LEARNING OUTCOMES	ASSESSMENT FOR LEARNING
I can talk about how I solve problems using counting.	How did you find out how many more pencils were needed so that children had one each?
I can count up to 20 objects. I know that the number of objects does not change even if I move the objects around. I can compare numbers up to 20 and say which number is bigger.	How many 10p coins are in the purse? How do you know you have that number? How do you know you have counted every coin? Would you rather have 9 pence or 15 pence? Why?

Resource links to existing published material

Mathematical challenges for able pupils Key Stages 1 and 2

ACTIVITIES
Four-pin bowling Activity 1
Gold Bars
Snakes and ladders

Intervention programmes

Springboard unit: None currently available

Supporting children with gaps in their mathematical understanding (Wave 3)

	Resource
Can only begin counting at 1; inaccurately counts objects when rearranged; has no consistent recognition of a small number of objects; lacks systematic approaches.	1 YR +/–

TABLE 6.1 Primary framework for literacy and mathematics: Year 1 Block A – Counting, partitioning and calculating Unit 1 (extract)

of any lesson or unit of work should also be differentiated, so as to use it to assess the success of individuals and groups in meeting particular learning objectives set for them. This too needs to be built into planning – not just what will be taught for children working outside age-related expectations, or how it will be taught, but also how it will be assessed.

Finally, SENCOs/INCOs may want to help colleagues think about ways of building children's *personal* targets into their planning. Tracked-back learning objectives work well for the majority of children with learning difficulties, for most of the time. However, as we saw in Chapter 5, there will be particular things that children with SEN or disabilities need to learn that are a real priority for their overall development, but may not always link to the class learning focus. As an example, the absolute priority for a child at a particular time might be to learn to take turns when sharing equipment, or to learn how to use question words when speaking. These are not targets that necessarily relate to learning objectives in a teacher's overall class planning. If a teacher was planning a mathematics lesson on measurement, for example, tracking back through the mathematics framework would not take them to learning objectives about taking turns or asking questions. It could be more important for her to think, in her planning, about how she could use the general context of the lesson to support the child's progress towards these priority personal targets. She might make a note in her planning, for example, to say that she would put the child in a group of three for a practical measuring activity, and explain to him beforehand that what she was looking for was to see him take turns with the measuring tape in the playground. If his target was to learn to ask questions featuring the question word 'what', she might make a note that in the plenary she would model the questions 'What did you do?' and 'What did you find out?' and then have the child put the questions to each group in turn.

Building personal learning targets into teachers' everyday planning in ways like this means that children with SEN or disabilities can do most of their learning with their peers, in the classroom, rather than be pulled out for separate IEP-related activities. It is like a child doing their special physiotherapy exercises in the context of a PE lesson, or their own special speech and language therapy activities in the context of mathematics or history.

This will not always be possible; sometimes it is simply more practical, economic and effective to provide the special learning that a child needs outside of the work of the class as a whole. An example might be a child with severe learning difficulties whose priority personal target is to learn how to cross the road safely, find the right bus home or pay the right fare. These would be occasions when separate planning would be appropriate, rather than trying to build the learning into the planning of class or subject teachers. Sometimes, we do try to stretch 'inclusion' (in the sense of being physically present in every mainstream lesson) too far.

Giangreco and his colleagues (1993) supply us with a vocabulary for thinking about planning for children with SEN or disabilities, which may be helpful to share with colleagues when training.

> Giangreco talks about four different options for student participation in general classroom activities.
>
> The first option he calls 'same'. This describes occasions when the student with SEN can pursue the same objectives and the same activities as others in the class. The example he gives is a lesson where a class is practising songs for a concert for parents.
>
> The second option is 'multi-level'. This is where students are all involved in a lesson in the same curriculum area but are pursuing different learning objectives at multiple levels based on their individual needs. This corresponds to the idea of tracking back (or forward) through relevant sequenced objectives such as those in national frameworks.
>
> The third option Giangreco calls *curriculum overlapping*. This occurs when a student with SEN is involved in the same lesson as the class, but is pursuing objectives from different curricular areas. This would correspond to the example of covering social/emotional or speech and language objectives in a maths lesson about measurement.
>
> Finally, Giangreco describes an option he calls 'alternative'. This refers to times when the regular class work does not offer reasonable opportunities to address the particular priority learning objectives for a student with SEN, and they need to be addressed discretely in a way that is not linked to the work of the class as a whole. It corresponds to the example of work on road safety and independent travel described above.

All teachers need to understand the difference between 'same', 'multi-level', 'overlapping' and 'alternative' learning objectives. They can then consider which of these options is most appropriate at any given time for a particular individual or group when planning. SENCOs/INCOs might want to help them by supplying a flow chart of questions, like the one in Figure 6.3.

 ## Access strategies

Having explained how everyday lesson planning can note tracked-back learning objectives for children with SEN or disabilities, or provide the

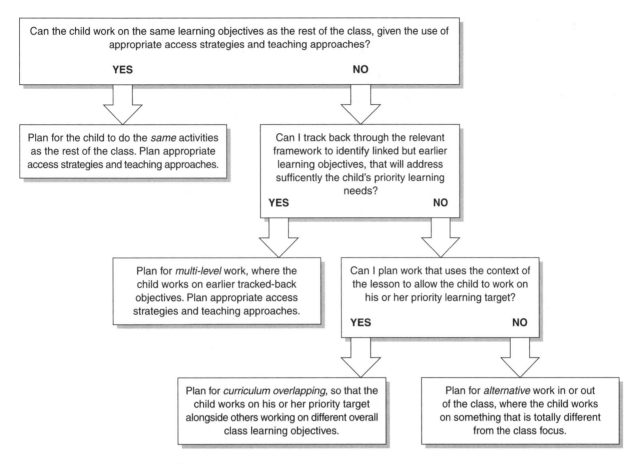

FIGURE 6.3 Questions flow chart

context for priority learning objectives that are not linked to those of the class as a whole, SENCOs/INCOs can go on to explore occasions when a child with SEN or disabilities *can* work on exactly the same learning objective as the rest of the group or class, if appropriate access strategies are deployed to overcome a barrier between the child and the learning.

A good example is that of a child with a visual impairment, but with no learning difficulties. Staff will readily agree that there is no reason for such a child to work on earlier learning objectives or be placed in a group of 'less able' children. If the barrier created by the visual impairment can be overcome by appropriate access strategies (by using an enlarged text, for example, or materials in Braille), the child can be expected to achieve the same learning objectives as their peers.

You could then ask staff what they would say about a bright child with behavioural difficulties – one with ADHD, for example. Does this child need work on earlier learning objectives? If he is placed with a group who are working at earlier levels (perhaps because they happen to have a TA with them), what are the implications for his learning? Are there any access strategies the teacher could implement to overcome the barriers to his own learning presented by this child's behaviour, and the learning of others? Ideas might be increased opportunities to be 'up and doing' rather than sitting, building in breaks when the child can for example take a message to another class or have a brief period of exercise, or providing an individual workstation that is screened at the sides.

Finally, you could ask staff to think about a child with dyslexic difficulties, who can express himself well orally and is quick to pick up new ideas. Do they think they need to plan for different learning objectives for him in science, maths, history, geography and so on? Does his slow reading, his brief and scrappy written work mean he is not capable of understanding the subject content of a lesson – or does it just mean that he needs access strategies that afford him scaffolded or alternative means of recording, such as those described in the toolkit section of this book? Are there subjects were he might need both differentiated learning objectives *and* access strategies? An example would be in English, where the class are working on spelling, and he does need to work on earlier learning objectives but might also need the access strategy of having a buddy read instructions on a spelling worksheet for him.

Questions like these, and the discussion they will prompt, will help colleagues to be aware that many underachieving children can work on the same learning objectives as others in the class, as long as the teacher plans access strategies to overcome a barrier between the child and the learning.

The idea of using access strategies extends to the whole area of inclusion, not just to SEN or disability. For EAL learners, the barrier might be difficulty in understanding the teacher's language as she explains a task. The access strategy might be simultaneous use of the child's home language. Or the teacher might plan to 'chunk' her speech into shorter sentences, illustrate it with pictures or real objects, and check on comprehension by asking the child to repeat the instruction back – all access strategies that would work equally well for a child in the class with speech and language difficulties. For gifted and talented pupils, the barrier might be the difference between the speed of their thoughts and their ability to get these thoughts onto paper. The teacher could overcome the barrier by suggesting the child uses concept mapping, for example, to get their ideas down quickly in a visual format. This strategy would work equally well for a dyslexic pupil in the class.

Access strategies should form part of every teacher's planning for personalised learning. Whenever they design tasks and activities for children, they need to be thinking about what might get in the way of learning, and be creative about ways around the barrier. What SENCOs/INCOs will want them to avoid is resorting to just one, not very creative access strategy – that of allocating a teaching assistant to support the group who are likely to have difficulties. This is the most common access strategy, but it places a heavy burden on the TA, who has to coax a group of children into completing tasks that have not been designed with their particular needs in mind, and may not even be addressing appropriate learning objectives.

 ## Teaching approaches

As well as planning access strategies to overcome specific barriers to learning, teachers need to think about the more general teaching approaches that are appropriate to particular types of SEN or disability.

Children with learning difficulties often benefit, for example, from teaching approaches which make abstract concepts real for them by making links to their everyday experiences. This is particularly so in mathematics, where building work on 'using and applying' into all lesson planning, rather than teaching it discretely, has been one of the benefits for children with SEN of the revised Primary Mathematics Framework.

These are some other examples of matching teaching approaches to particular needs:

- Children on the autistic spectrum benefit from visual approaches – props serving to back up a story or an explanation, and visual timetables that give a sense of routine and help them understand what will be expected of them and when.
- Children whose behaviour presents challenges may benefit from absolute clarity about what is expected of them, and opportunities for active and interactive learning that involves them in 'doing' rather than sitting passively.
- Children with learning difficulties or those on the autistic spectrum might

need tasks that are relatively closed – that is, where the task is structured for them and they do not have to invent their own ways of going about it ('Follow the step-by-step instructions on the card…'). This might contrast with the need of more able children to tackle tasks that are more open-ended or extended in time ('Devise your own experiment to explore friction').

Drawing on a variety of teaching styles and approaches (open and closed tasks, short and long tasks, visual, auditory or kinaesthetic learning) matched to the needs of individuals forms the background to planning for both teacher exposition and independent or group activities.

Planning a staff meeting or part of an INSET day

The first step, then, for SENCOs/INCOs who want to influence teachers' planning is to provide training, either at a staff meeting or as part of an INSET day, on the 'three circles' model – getting the learning objectives right, planning specific access strategies to overcome barriers to learning, and drawing on a variety of teaching styles and approaches.

Materials for such training are available on the DVD *Leading on intervention* (DfES, 2006d). They are designed for primary schools but could readily be adapted by a secondary SENCO. They include a handout on the three circles model and a range of discussion questions, for example those in Figure 6.4 below.

Teachers go on to work in year group or class teams and consider a child with SEN or a child whose behaviour presents barriers to learning. They

FIGURE 6.4 Example discussion questions

share an example of short-term planning they have brought with them, together identify the appropriate learning objectives for the child, any teaching styles or approaches that might be particularly effective, and any specific barriers that might need to be overcome in order to make sure the child can access the learning objectives, using a checklist of inclusive teaching strategies as a prompt. Groups feed back their best idea for an access strategy or teaching approach.

Training like this should include teaching assistants wherever possible, and should tackle the issue of communicating planning to the TA or TAs who are working with a class. In the most effective schools, TAs take an active part in departmental and lesson planning, and can often contribute a specialist knowledge about access strategies and teaching approaches that will work for a particular type of SEN or a particular pupil. They cannot be expected to supply effective support unless they know in advance what the pupils are to learn (the learning objectives for the class as a whole and for the pupils they are supporting) and what their role is to be. At Coombe Boys' School, the case study school we met in Chapter 2, TAs are given teachers' planners and a checklist of information to be stored in these. The information includes schemes of work, short- and long-term curriculum plans and class lists with annotated needs.

 ## Planning formats

Having provided staff with a conceptual model to help them think about differentiating their planning, the next step might be to consult with them on modifications to the existing planning formats operating in the school.

It will be important to reassure colleagues that they are not being asked to write separate plans for all the children in a class. The government document *Making good progress* puts this well:

> The personalised classroom does not entail having up to 30 separate teaching plans; it is about having one strong inclusive teaching plan which allows as much room as possible for individual engagement, targeted support, a degree of choice and respect for the range of abilities and interests in the class.
>
> (DfES, 2007)

Staff might decide that planning formats should include a dedicated space

TEACHER:			SUBJECT: English	DATE
Class: 9 L	NOR: 23	Grouping: mixed ability	NC Levels: 2–7	
Unit of work: Study of Key Stage 3 Shakespeare text				

Objectives (WALT)	Outcomes (WILF)
Read and understand key scene from text. Explore characters and what motivates them.	Brief monologues (soliloquies) that give a good picture of the opinions and feelings of one character. Complete reading of key scene from set text; understanding of what has happened and why.

Activities	Differentiation (SEN/G and T/EAL)
Starter Paired recap on previous lesson's reading – key actions/characters. Q and A by teacher.	Pupils to work in their buddy (mixed ability) pairs. Ask Qs using 'infer', 'speculate' to challenge more able.
Main Use IWB to display a usual wedding and contrast with play. Display still from movie – identify main characters. Individuals choose one character and write brief monologue exploring the character's thoughts and feelings in the scene. Paired work – read and comment on each other's monologue Complete reading of scene with individuals taking parts, up to Leonardo's losing control.	Give Ian, Parin, Anthony a copy of the last IWB slide (the still) with starter ideas in boxes for each character – students to choose one and complete in the box. Dan to work with Robbie – Robbie scribe. Pupils to work in regular (ability-matched) pairs.
Plenary What will be the effect of the scene on events to come? Last IWB slide – have students add thought bubbles for all main characters.	
Assessment opportunities Use plenary to check understanding for five target pupils.	
Homework Edit your monologue in the light of others' comments/ what actually happened in the scene.	Ian, Parin, Anthony to read instead next two scenes in Comic Book Shakespeare (www.shakespearecomics.com) in preparation for next lesson.

TABLE 6.2 Lesson plan

Unit: ....   **Date:** ....   **Year group:** ....

Key learning objectives: ....

Learning outcome for unit: ....

Planning for inclusion – note here differentiated learning objectives for different individuals and groups, and the teaching approaches and access strategies you will use to overcome barriers to learning.

FIGURE 6.5 Example planning format

(extra boxes, columns or rows) on which they can note particular adaptations to be made for pupils with SEN or disabilities, more able pupils or other groups such as EAL learners. Table 6.2 shows an example for the secondary phase; Table 2.2 in Chapter 2 one for the primary phase.

Or staff might decide to add a blank version of the three overlapping circles to the school's planning format, so that they can write in any learning objectives different from those for the class as a whole, any particular teaching approaches they will adopt to meet the needs of individuals, and any access strategies required (Figure 6.5).

Another idea might be for the SENCO/INCO to add a standard extra box to the planning format, containing a list of inclusive teaching strategies applicable to a wide range of special or individual needs. When planning for a particular class, the class or subject teacher simply has to reflect on needs present in the group and tick or highlight the strategies they want to make sure they apply. A possible model for this appears in the toolkit section of this book.

A final option is simply annotating existing printed plans by hand or electronically, to note the adaptations that will be made to meet the needs

Medium-term Plan Subject: ITC Branching databases (Flexi Tree) Term: Spring

Key Questions/Activity List	Resources	Teaching and learning intention and how it will be assessed
Show the class a selection of about eight materials, such as marbles, water, oil, salt. Tell the class that you are thinking of one of the objects, and that they must work out which one it is by asking 'yes/no' questions, such as 'Is it a solid?' Discuss which questions work well and point out that questions about small numbers of objects are unhelpful if the answer is no. Encourage them to use questions which divide the set of objects into two. Show the class how to create a tree diagram of branching questions, which can be used to identify each object. Do on IWB. Divide the class into mixed ability groups; give each group a tree diagram challenge. e.g. use a tree diagram to separate the Tudor monarchs.	Selection of about six materials such as marbles, water, oil, salt. 'Big' and smaller paper trees.	The children will be able to create Y/N questions to categorise information.
Create a branching database in order to create a database to classify different organisms, e.g. Lives on land?	7 different organisms. Pics from science week. Paper tree. Labels, wordbank.	The children will be able to use their knowledge of branching databases to create a database to classify organisms

Annotations (callouts):

- *TP KS MM MLG to do four objects with CT support.*
- *JH RLG practice yes/no questions about people and sort selves before joining the group.*
- *Plus group of TP/KS/MM/ML G/JH/RLG*
- *ML, NG To relate back to science and use appropriate vocabulary. ML, AW – HA in history. Higher order questions What if ...?*
- *ML, NG include more organisms (with obvious similarities) in order to make the task more challenging. Where would you put a frog? Why? ML ...?*
- *JH, RLG – to have time prior to session with ICT buddy with 1:1 support in setting up a branching database (and after, to consolidate).*
- *JH, RLG, TP, KS, MM, MLG with CT recap on pics from science earlier in term linked to animal attributes and habitats. Sort 4 on paper tree before transferring onto computer (labels, spellings provided).*

FIGURE 6.6 Planning annotated for children with SEN and more able of particular groups or individuals. Figure 6.6 gives an example, for an ICT unit of work in a class which includes children with speech and language needs, children with difficulties in cognition and learning, and several highly able pupils.

The process of planning for individuals in the context of the class is becoming increasingly easy as tools such as the interactive planning tool within the electronic Primary Framework become available. Such tools allow teachers to do multi-level planning by pulling down into their planning objectives from earlier or later year groups. They allow teachers to cut and paste in questions at different levels that can help them to assess whether individual children have reached learning objectives. Plans that are saved from year to year can readily be amended to include teaching approaches and access strategies appropriate for the particular needs of 'this year's class'. Those teaching approaches and access strategies can be cut and pasted across from subject to subject, saving time and helping to ensure that ideas added to one plan as a result of a discussion with the SENCO/INCO or an outside agency will be applied more widely.

When thinking as a staff about how they want to record differentiation on their planning, it is important to avoid people making a rod for their own backs by trying to record every detail of the inclusive teaching approaches they practise with a class. Planning is there to guide teaching and assessment, and what goes on it should only be what the teacher needs as a prompt. A teacher who has taught a number of children with autism, for example, is likely to have internalised the sorts of strategies that will be helpful and will automatically employ visual supports and closed rather than open-ended assessment tasks. The teacher does not need to annotate their planning to that effect. A teacher new to autism, however, might need to record explicitly on her planning a reminder to herself to do these things.

In general the minimum that might be recorded by all teachers is:

- the appropriate tracked-back (or -forward) learning objectives for a particular group or, if the class contains children working well below age-related expectations, for one or two individuals;
- the different tasks that groups or individuals will be set, including any different homework;

- what will happen in the plenary to enable children working on different objectives to demonstrate their learning;
- one or more questions the teacher will ask to assess understanding.

 ## Modelling and coaching

Agreed inclusive planning formats can be helpful in guiding teachers towards appropriate differentiation. As ever, however, it is the *process* used to support teachers' planning that is more important than what ends up being written down. The most productive processes involve the SENCO or INCO in collaborative planning with class or subject teachers. The SENCO/INCO acts as consultant to the teacher, listening to the outline of what they want to teach and making suggestions about learning objectives, teaching approaches and access strategies that are appropriate for children in the class who have SEN or disabilities.

The examples that follow show how this can be done.

PLANNING EXAMPLE

Planning collaboratively with a Year 3 class teacher

A Year 3 teacher was planning work on speaking and listening, using a Qualifications and Curriculum Authority (QCA) unit in which children discuss different scenarios for an ending to a novel they have been reading (*The Battle of Bubble and Squeak* by Philippa Pearce), and decide which is the most plausible. The lesson objective was to use the language of possibility to investigate and reflect on feelings, behaviour or relationships. Children were going to discuss how to talk about things which 'might' happen, incorporating words like 'may', might', 'could', 'perhaps', then work in groups to talk about different endings to the story, and have a spokesperson to report on their discussion.

The class contained a number of children with speech and language difficulties, so their teacher asked for the SENCO's help in planning adaptations she could make to meet their needs.

The first step was to consider whether the teacher would need to track back to earlier learning objectives for some children. Two of the children were able to express themselves only in simple sentences, and had been assessed as working at P6–7 in speaking and listening. The SENCO suggested that an appropriate

---

objective for them would still involve the language of prediction, but at a simpler level – learning to understand and use words like 'guess', 'I think', 'I don't know.'

SENCO and class teacher then discussed how this learning objective could be brought in to the lesson introduction, in which the teacher was going to explain to the children that we use different language to talk about things which might happen, rather than things we are sure about. The teacher then wanted to ask the class questions about what they had done in the morning before they came to school, and what they might do after school – using language like 'Are you sure?', 'Is that definite?' to generate vocabulary expressing possibility.

The teacher thought she could bring in the learning objectives for the children with language difficulties here. With the help of the SENCO, she decided to display a covered box right at the start of the lesson and ask the children if they knew what was in it, then produce two pictures and ask them to guess which one might be inside the box. This would allow her to highlight words like 'guess', 'know', 'don't know', 'think'.

The next step was to think about any access strategies that children with SEN might need after the lesson introduction. The SENCO suggested that she might employ play people and small models, or a story sack of concrete objects to support her recap of the *The Battle of Bubble and Squeak* so far, as the language would present a barrier to the children with communication difficulties, and also to EAL learners in the group.

For the group work part of the lesson, the teacher planned to give each group a different story prediction/ending to work on, and ask them to talk about how likely their ending might be, using the clues from the story so far. She wanted the children with communication difficulties to take part, so that they could have access to the role models provided by other children's language, but decided to give them a clear role – that of timekeeper for their group.

In the plenary she wanted to return both to the overall class learning objective and to the specific objectives she had planned for the children with communication difficulties. The SENCO suggested that she might hold a class vote on which of the different possible endings would be the one in the final chapter of the book. The spokesperson for each group would hold up a card with 'their' ending drawn on it, and children would be asked to go and stand by the ending they thought most likely. First, though, she would ask the children with communication needs to 'guess' which ending would win, encouraging them to repeat and complete the sentence 'I guess that...'. For other children, she would use the language of 'predict', 'might', 'perhaps' and so on.

PLANNING EXAMPLE

Planning collaboratively for a Year 7 history lesson

This class was a mixed ability Year 7 group, in which eight pupils had learning difficulties and two had been formally identified as dyslexic. They had been learning in history about native Americans. The school's SENCO had allocated time to work intensively with members of the history department, modelling for them how planning could be adapted to take account of a range of SEN and disabilities. He sat down with the teacher working with this Year 7 group and established what the learning objective was for the class – on this occasion to understand how important the buffalo was to the survival of the native Americans. They agreed that this objective was appropriate for all the children, including those with learning difficulties, as long as appropriate teaching approaches and access strategies were deployed.

Multisensory teaching approaches are important for children with difficulties in cognition and learning, and this was easy to plan as staff had already had training in using VAK (visual, auditory and kinaesthetic) methods. The teacher had therefore already planned to feature visual materials – a Powerpoint presentation on the interactive whiteboard that illustrated key information.

The SENCO suggested that the teacher put a list of key words on the wall ('nomadic', 'tribe', 'buffalo' and so on) and that she reinforce these in the whiteboard presentation for the benefit of children with reading difficulties.

The lesson was to involve children in writing down what they thought each part of a buffalo (hide, fat, teeth and so on) might be used for. The SENCO suggested supporting those with learning difficulties here by operating a buddy system. The seating plan would pair children who found writing difficult with those who wrote fluently (but might not always have good ideas). Children would be asked to talk in these buddy pairs then have the better writer record their initial ideas, to feed back in the class discussion.

Managing to get homework down quickly can be a problem for dyslexic children, and understanding what they have to do in their homework a problem for children with general learning difficulties. The SENCO had been working for some time with staff to get them to spend more time explaining homework, and to give it to children in handout form rather than expecting them to copy it down quickly from the board at the end of the lesson.

He discussed how this could happen in the history lesson, with the teacher perhaps giving the children a homework sheet in the middle of the lesson, and rehearsing with them what they would have to do. This was a good point to suggest, too, that handouts on buff paper in a font like Arial would add to their readability for dyslexic pupils. The SENCO and teacher looked together at how the homework handout could be differentiated by providing some pupils with a box of key words on their sheet, or by giving them part-completed sentences to finish.

The SENCO also suggested that, in the part of the lesson where pupils had discussed their initial ideas on the use of various parts of the buffalo, watched a further presentation from the teacher, and were writing up their learning, some children might use a laptop with software installed that enabled text to be read aloud. The laptop would be supplied by the learning support department.

The SENCO and teacher then briefly discussed ways of involving children with learning difficulties in a plenary. The SENCO learned that this teacher regularly employed strategies to help less confident children answer questions. In this lesson, for example, he planned to make sure that lower-attaining children had their chance to come up to the whiteboard and drag words into the right places in sentences about the buffalo – but if they struggled, would be ready to offer them the chance to 'phone a friend' or 'ask the audience'.

The advantages of a collaborative planning process like the one featured in these examples are that the process makes strategies for children with SEN and disabilities live and real for class and subject teachers. The conversation concerns the specific content that the teacher is actually going to work on with a class. The ideas generated are therefore likely to be deployed, and remembered. Training provides the groundwork, but collaborative planning translates ideas into action.

Collaborative planning also leaves something behind. Every minute the SENCO/INCO invests in it will have a pay-off far beyond the children involved in the immediate piece of teaching. The joint planning supplies the teacher with ideas that they can use again and again in the future, even when the SENCO/INCO is not supporting them directly.

For children with the more common types of SEN or disability, like general learning difficulties, specific learning difficulties or mild behaviour difficulties, the SENCO/INCO may not need to invest very much time before teacher colleagues are able to incorporate appropriate differentiation into their everyday planning. The strategy sheets included in the toolkit section of this book may be all they need to keep them going.

Where children have less common or more complex needs – for example, children with sensory impairment, or those with severe learning difficulties who will function at or below Level 2 of the National Curriculum throughout their school career, the involvement of the SENCO/INCO or outside agencies will continue to be needed. A primary class teacher working with a child who has little or no sight, for example, should expect to be able to sit down with a specialist teacher of the visually impaired and look in advance at medium-term planning, so that the specialist teacher can advise on access strategies and help in the preparation of appropriate resources.

Similarly, if a child has severe learning difficulties and is working at levels very significantly below those of the class as a whole, there will be a need to identify in medium-term planning those learning opportunities in which the child can profitably take part, working on either tracked-back learning objectives linked to those of the class as a whole, or on separate objectives (curriculum overlapping).

The examples that follow illustrate this process.

PLANNING EXAMPLE

Planning collaboratively for a Year 4 science lesson

This example describes how a teacher planned for a Year 4 class with diverse needs that included one child with profound and multiple learning difficulties. In science, he was planning work on temperature, involving the use of an electronic thermometer/probe. The children were to predict then measure the temperature of various liquids. Clearly the science learning objectives were not relevant to the needs of Shamina, the child with profound and multiple learning difficulties, whose learning was at a very early developmental level.

The teacher had access to advice from a teacher from a local special school and discussed with her how he might adapt his planning. The specialist teacher used the idea of curriculum overlapping, to show how the child with profound learning difficulties could be involved in the class activities, but for the primary purpose of pursuing objectives from other curriculum areas – in this case, communication. The objective would be for Shamina to begin to link the words 'hot' and 'cold' with the relevant sensory experience. Appropriate teaching approaches for a child working at this level would need to be based on concrete materials that generate a strong sensory stimulus.

The class teacher suggested that they use two hot water bottles, one filled with hot and one with icy water. A TA would work with Shamina and three other children, encouraging them to first let Shamina feel each of the hot water bottles and hear the words for each of them, then try to engage her in anticipation (an early cognitive forerunner of prediction) by saying 'Ready, it's going to be **cold**' or 'Ready, it's going to be **hot**.' The more able children would then predict the temperature in each of the bottles and measure it with a probe. Assessment would involve the TA in videoing Shamina's responses, looking for any sign of anticipation.

PLANNING EXAMPLE

Planning collaboratively across the curriculum

Globetown Action Zone, a partnership between five schools in East London working to raise standards through support for vulnerable groups, received funding for a curriculum development project. They decided to use the funding to work on differentiated planning with subject faculties in one secondary school. Teachers' planning had so far differentiated only down to NC Level 3 in Year 7, but not below this.

The project involved skilled teachers with prior experience in the relevant faculty, and often with early years and primary teaching experience also. These teachers were asked to 'track' each scheme or unit of work and prepare lesson-by-lesson plans for work appropriate for pupils working below Level 2 when they moved to secondary at the age of 11. The schemes of work now take pupils with learning difficulties from 'P' scale levels in Year 7 through to Year 11 work that can potentially consolidate Level 3 and begin Level 4. Maths, geography, history, RE and English are covered.

In maths, for example, a Year 8 scheme of work involved the class in working on position (coordinates), straight-line graphs and expressing simple functions in words. For one lesson these objectives were tracked back (using multi-level planning) to the use of everyday words to describe position and direction. Pupils with learning difficulties worked on the key words 'column', 'row', 'left', 'right' and 'position' during a game they played in pairs – each moving counters on a grid and answering the question 'What's your position?' The planning includes questions that the class teacher can pose to involve everyone during the plenary, such as 'Can you write instructions using shorthand, for example 2R (move 2 squares to the right)?'

In geography, a potentially challenging lesson on tectonics was made accessible by planning for pupils with learning difficulties to use a simple instruction sheet to construct an 'edible earth' consisting of crust, mantle, outer core and inner core, using three different colours of ice cream, nuts and edible silver spheres. In the plenary they had to identify each part as they ate their edible earth, sharing it with the class.

In history, a Year 9 scheme of work on women at work in World War I involved the class in studying the impact of the war on the changing roles of women. In planning for differentiation, it was decided that pupils with learning difficulties could access the same learning objectives as the class, as long as particular teaching approaches and access strategies were employed. These involved adding picture supports to information sheets, in the form of black-and-white photographs of women as bus conductors, nurses, farmworkers and so on. Worksheets were simplified and supports provided in the form of sentence starters and picture–word matching activities. The teachers also took the opportunity to develop work on a key life skill for pupils with learning difficulties (writing a CV and job application) in parallel to the main history objectives (curriculum overlapping again). Pupils had to choose a job that supported the war effort and construct a letter of application composed of the cut-up sentence starters and key job vocabulary. Pupils also constructed their own CV incorporating a digital photograph of themselves.

Table 6.3 shows some of the resources that were developed to support this history scheme of work.

Topic: Women at work in World War I 1914–1918.

Lesson 1: What jobs did women do in World War 1?

Main lesson objective	• To understand the importance of women in World War I.
Key words	• Jobs, employment, transport, factories, farms, nursing.
Activities for pupils with learning difficulties	• Read through fact sheet on World War I. • Explain that at this time only men could do manual jobs. However, when the men went to war women were needed to carry out the jobs previously done by the men. Harvest was completed by women, nurses cared for soldiers, and women worked in factories and took over transport. • Look at pictures and discuss the work that is going on. • Match the sentences to the pictures.
Resources	• Information sheet • Worksheet 1 • Set of laminated pictures • Set of laminated sentences
Plenary	• Ask the children what job they would have volunteered for if they had been alive in 1914–1918.

Lesson 1
Information sheet
Woman at work during World War I
(1914–1918)

What jobs did women do in World War I?
During World War I 9 million men were mobilised in Britain and the Empire.
The government needed women in Britain to carry out manual tasks.

- Women found employment in transport. They drove buses and trams.
- They worked in nursing.
- Women found work in factories making ammunition.
- Women had to work on farms to harvest the food.
- Some women had to drive trucks.

These were all jobs that only men had done before the war. Women proved that they could do these jobs as well as the men.

Lesson 1
Worksheet 1

Woman at work during World War I:
- Look at the pictures and discuss what you can see.
- Why are the pictures in black and white?
- What are the jobs that the women are doing?
- Can you match the sentences to the pictures?
- What job would you have chosen to do?

TABLE 6.3 Resources for a Year 9 history scheme of work at Morpeth school

Lesson 2: What job would you apply for to help in the war?

Main lesson objective	• (Class)To understand the types of jobs that supported the war effort. • (Pupils with learning difficulties)To write an application for a job using Curriculum Vitae.
Key words	• Jobs, employment, transport, Curriculum Vitae, farms, nursing.
Activities for pupils with learning difficulties	• Discuss with the pupils what job they would like to do to support the war effort. • Remind them that this would be the first time women would be allowed to work in manual jobs. • Read through Worksheet 1. • Explain that Worksheet 2 gives words and sentence starters to help with their writing. • Pupils to cut out and match words and then complete own writing. • Pupils will fill in Curriculum Vitae (Worksheet 3) giving information about themselves.
Resources	• Information sheet • Worksheet 1 • Set of laminated pictures from week 1 • Digital photo of each pupil • Worksheet 2, cut-up words • Worksheet 3
Plenary	• To share writing with the class.

Lesson 2
Worksheet 1
• When you want to get a job it is necessary for you to complete an application form.
• Once you have decided which job you would like to do then you will have to complete a CV. This is short for Curriculum Vitae.
• A CV gives employers information about you, including:

  • your name;
  • when you were born (date of birth);
  • your home address or your school address;
  • what type of person you are;
  • any qualifications;
  • hobbies or interests.

Remember you can choose a job from the pictures that you have in front of you.

TABLE 6.3 Continued

Lesson 2
Worksheet 2

I would like to be a _____

I would be good at _____

because _____

I am _____

hardworking

kind

caring

nurse

truck driver

bus conductor

farm worker

motor cyclist

Lesson 2
Worksheet 3
CV
Name: _____ Photograph:

Date of birth: (day, month, year)

_____

Address:

_____

_____

My hobbies:

_____

_____

What job would you like to do?

_____
_____
_____
_____

TABLE 6.3 Continued

Monitoring

So far we have looked at how a SENCO or INCO might help in training colleagues in how to plan for a range of needs in their class, and how to support this through opportunities for collaborative planning – for modelling and coaching. Ideally, there would also be chances from time to time to follow up collaborative planning with review. 'How did the lesson go?', the SENCO might ask. 'How did those with SEN or disabilities respond? What worked and what didn't? What strategies might you want to use again or apply in other subjects or with other age groups?'

If change is to be embedded, however, it will also need to be monitored, and built into existing performance management systems. Teachers might for a period all have a target to increase the amount and quality of differentiation in their planning. This could form part of the school's curriculum access plan or (better and less bureaucratic) part of a section of the school development or improvement plan concerned with increasing curriculum access.

Monitoring is relatively straightforward. From time to time the SENCO/INCO looks at a sample of planning drawn from across the school, and supplies feedback to individual staff and an overview for the senior leadership team and subject leaders of issues arising from the monitoring exercise. The subject or whole-school issues unearthed will feed into school self-evaluation and the SEF. Any issues relating to individuals feed into performance management and the provision of extra training and support. A suggested monitoring proforma appears in the toolkit section of this book.

Finally, the school will want to know whether its improved planning is feeding through into teaching. Whoever is monitoring teaching in the school – members of SMT, subject leaders, the SENCO/INCO when gathering specific evidence on SEN and disability for the SEF – will need to check whether there is a clear read-through from planning through to what they see happening in the classroom for children with additional needs.

Achieving Targets
Mapping Additional Provision

So far, we have looked at a number of key elements of our essential bureaucracy-busting kit that constitutes an alternative to writing individual plans for every child with SEN or a disability – at Personal Profiles, whole-school target-setting and tracking systems, and differentiated curriculum planning. In this chapter we tackle another element, provision maps.

Provision maps were described in *Special educational needs and school improvement* (Gross and White, 2003), with further guidance outlined since then in the National Strategies' materials *Leading on inclusion* (DfES, 2005c), *Leading on intervention* (DfES, 2006d) and *Effective leadership: ensuring the progress of pupils with SEN and/or disabilities* (DfES, 2006a). It is not the intention to repeat this information here. For those who may not be familiar with the concept, this chapter will briefly summarise what a provision map is and the function it fulfils, but the main focus will be on what has been learned since more and more schools began to take on provision mapping. We will look at what to do to keep the process of developing a provision map as simple as possible, how to build new developments into quality interventions, and how to move from effective provision mapping to effective provision management.

What is a provision map?

A provision map is a way of describing the provision that a school makes for children with additional needs, over and above inclusive class or subject teaching, using additional targeted time from teachers, teaching assistants or volunteers.

Table 7.1 presents an example of a primary provision map, and Table 7.2 a secondary map. Provision is best mapped by year group (although in very small schools it might be mapped by phase) and by types of provision – literacy interventions, mathematics interventions, interventions to boost oral language skills, motor coordination or social, emotional and behavioural

PROVISION	YR	Y1	Y2	Y3	Y4	Y5	Y6
Language intervention		*Talking Partners*					
Literacy intervention	Phonological awareness group	*Reading Recovery FFT Wave 3 ELS*	Y6 buddy readers (*Better Reading Partnership*)	*Year 3 Literacy Support (Y3LS)* Y6 buddy readers (*Better Reading Partnership*)	Y6 buddy readers (*Better Reading Partnership*)	*Further Literacy Support* Paired reading programme Reciprocal teaching	Paired reading programme
Maths intervention			*Numeracy Recovery*		Teacher and TA – Primary Strategy Wave 3 materials	Teacher and TA – Primary Strategy Wave 3 materials *Springboard 5*	Teacher and TA – Primary Strategy Wave 3 materials
Coordination programme		Weekly breakfast group plus home programme					
EAL provision	Home language support and additional language work for early stage learners	Home language support, pre-tutoring and additional language work for early stage learners	Home language support, pre-tutoring and additional language work for early stage learners	Small group language enrichment and pre-tutoring for children at later stages of learning EAL	Small group language enrichment and pre-tutoring for children at later stages of learning EAL	Small group language enrichment and pre-tutoring for children at later stages of learning EAL	Small group language enrichment and pre-tutoring for children at later stages of learning EAL
1–1 counselling/ solution focused work with learning mentor	Estimated 3 pupils per year group						

Achieving Targets: Additional Provision

Small group SEAL work	Nurture group	SEAL silver sets	SEAL silver sets Circle of Friends	Pyramid Club SEAL Silver sets	SEAL Silver sets	SEAL Silver sets	Transition group
In-class support							
Attendance	Walking bus					Learning mentor programme targeting attendance/ engagement	Learning mentor programme targeting attendance/ engagement
Gifted and talented provision				After-school clubs with secondary buddies			
Other	1–1 work with TA on programme devised by speech and language therapist	1–1 TA work with child with ASD on social scripts	1–1 TA sensory programme supervised through outreach from SLD special school	1–1 work with TA on programme devised by speech and language therapist	ASD social skills group		

TABLE 7.1 Example of a primary provision map

PROVISION	Y7	Y8	Y9	Y10	Y11
Targeted literacy intervention	*Literacy progress units* – 4 groups (pupils <L4) *Reading and Writing Challenge* with librarian – 5 pupils	*Reading and Writing Challenge* with librarian – 5 pupils			
Targeted maths intervention	*Springboard 7* (pupils <L4) – 5 groups,	*Maths Challenge* 1–1 with maths TA			
Targeted science intervention		*Science intervention* – TA in class group	*Science intervention* – TA in class group		
Further SEN literacy intervention	*Toe by Toe* programme 1–1 with teacher (pupils <L3) Early morning reading club	*Paired reading* programme organised by inclusion coordinator, involving disaffected Year 10 as tutors – approx. 18 pupils involved on a rolling programme Lunchtime literacy computer programmes, in library		Lunchtime literacy computer programmes, in library	
Further SEN mathematics intervention	SEN teacher – Primary Strategy Wave 3 materials with 7 pupils	SEN teacher – Primary Strategy Wave 3 materials with 6 pupils			
EAL provision	*Grammar for Writing* – group of advanced bilingual learners – English teacher with support from EMA teacher	Home language support and additional language work for 2 children at the early stages of learning EAL	Home language support and additional language work for 4 children at the early stages of learning EAL	Additional language work and academic tutoring for an estimated 3 new arrivals	Additional language work and academic tutoring for an estimated 3 new arrivals
1–1 counselling	Via Learning Support unit (LSU) team – estimated 12 pupils per year group				

Focus group work to develop social, emotional and behavioural skills	*Nurture group* for 8 pupils entering Y7	*Circle of Friends* for 3 pupils	SEAL friendship skills focus group and 2 anger management groups run by LSU team Lunchtime club		
1–1 mentoring to increase aspirations/ engagement with learning	*Learning Challenge* 1–1 with Learning Mentor Buddy system Y7–Y12 organised by Learning Mentor	*Learning Challenge* 1–1 with Learning Mentor		Learning Mentors work on programme targeting attendance/engagement Success group for Black Caribbean boys	Learning Mentors work on programme targeting attendance/engagement
In-class support for individuals	*Kalam, Jamila, Jenny, Cameron, David*	*John, Rafiq, Attia, Brendan*	*Stephen, Adam, Parvis, Aki, Jahangir, Sedef*	*Gareth, Brooke*	*William B, Patrick, Travis, Sara*
Extended school offer	Homework/ICT club	Homework/ICT club	Homework/ICT club Outdoor activity programme for targeted pupils	Study support tutorials ICT room group	Study support tutorials ICT room group
Gifted and talented provision	Specialist lunchtime enrichment clubs			Mentoring by university students	
Other	1–1 work with TA on programme devised by speech and language therapist – *Cameron* 1–1 TA work with child with ASD on social scripts – *David* Touchtyping – 2 pupils (20 mins, during registration)	1–1 TA work with child with ASD on social scripts *Anthony, Rafiq, Brendan* Social skills group work with this group	1–1 TA sensory programme supervised through outreach from SLD special school *Beth*	Tailored curriculum group of 12 – Youth Awards, vocational programme, Certificate of Achievement in English and Maths	

TABLE 7.2 Example of a secondary provision map

skills. It can also be helpful to subdivide literacy and mathematics provision into 'Wave 2' and 'Wave 3' interventions. This will distinguish the provision made for different target groups – those who are working just below age-related expectations and can be expected to catch up with their peers as a result of a tightly structured programme of small group support delivered by adults working to a script (Wave 2), and those for whom the gap is wider, and who will need one-to-one or very small group support from a specialist teacher or highly trained teaching assistant able to design learning experiences tailored to the assessed needs of the child (Wave 3). Schools that make extensive provision for children with social, emotional and behavioural needs often find it helpful to subdivide their provision in this area into 'Wave 2' and 'Wave 3' also.

It is good practice to include in a provision map all the different types of additional support a school offers children – whether they be in need of booster or catch-up assistance, identified as having SEN, EAL learners, gifted or talented, presenting behaviour difficulties or vulnerable for other reasons. This saves the time, paper and effort that might be spent on constructing separate maps for different types of need. It recognises the overlap between needs, in which a child with autism taking part in a social skills group might also require support as an EAL learner. Most importantly, it allows the school to achieve an overview of all the additional needs in each year group and make a coherent plan to meet them.

In so doing, it enables the SENCO/INCO to follow the general principle that forms the core message of this book – that children with SEN or disabilities are better served by integrated systems that personalise learning for all children, rather than separate systems that are driven by SEN categories and procedures.

Steps in developing a provision map

The steps involved in developing a provision map are shown in Figure 7.1.

Auditing the projected need in each year group in the next school year means listing types of provision you could make: literacy, mathematics, language, social and emotional, motor coordination, EAL/EMA, attendance and gifted and talented provision, and an 'other 'heading to cover very individual arrangements made for children with less common types of SEN. Then under each you write the names of children for whom that additional

FIGURE 7.1 Steps involved in developing a provision map

provision would be desirable. It is helpful if on your lists (perhaps shown by a particular colour) you distinguish those for whom additional provision is essential – for example, children with Statements specifying a particular provision, or children at a very early stage of English-language acquisition. You might also choose to list provisions for children at School Action Plus as essential. Next, enter in another colour those who have the next highest call on available provision. These could be children whose difficulties impact very significantly on their own or others' learning or those who have the potential, with relatively little help, to catch up with their peers and achieve age-related expectations in social and emotional learning, literacy or mathematics. Finally, enter the names of children for whom you make additional provision, if the budget allows, but for whom the priority is lower.

Comparing projected year group needs with current provision and identifying changes and staff development needs means looking at the audit you have done for each year group for the coming school year and noticing differences between the audit and current needs and provision in that year group. Is there going to be an increase in children in Year 1 who need support to develop their speech and language skills, for example, that might mean introducing a new intervention and training staff (in advance) to implement it? Will there still be a group needing to do the Primary Strategy Year 3 literacy support programme, or not? What does the incoming Year 7 look like in terms of need for literacy progress units, maths Springboard 7 and Wave 3 mathematics support? Does it contain a number of children on the autistic spectrum and, if so what are the implications for provision and staff development? Does next year's Year 9 have a large group of pupils who, according to current tracking, are making poor progress across the board, because of lack of engagement with learning and, if so, is a mentoring programme required?

Identifying the available school budget means pulling together different funding streams, such as a core amount from the school's base budget, delegated SEN funding, EMA funding, specific government grants for personalisation, and local authority funding for priorities such as early intervention or behaviour support. It will be necessary to ring-fence any funding that is allocated through a Statement of SEN which specifies that the child must receive a fixed number of hours of TA support or other specified assistance. Otherwise, funding streams should be combined so as to achieve the best possible fit to the priorities identified in the audit. Coherently planned provision which draws together a range of funding sources is more likely to achieve positive outcomes than piecemeal use of pockets of money.

The next step, *considering the evidence on what works*, means making choices about which interventions you will put on next year's provision map, drawing on information produced nationally (in materials such as the DfES (2006d) *Leading on intervention* CD), by your local authority, from your own research and reading and from your evaluation of interventions previously attempted in school.

Once the map has been drawn up and the new school year has begun, precise tracking information can be used to *match children to the appropriate provision*. This process will be easier, and fairer, if you have established clear entry and exit criteria for each of your provisions. Finally, 'before' and 'after' measures can serve to *track children's progress* as a result of the intervention, and this information used to *evaluate the impact of each provision*. This in turn feeds back into the provision-mapping cycle, helping to inform your choice of interventions in the future.

What are provision maps for?

A provision map is fundamentally a management tool, based on auditing the needs of year groups, deciding as a result what provision is needed in which year groups, and using this to determine budgetary and staffing arrangements. Its main value is 'the strategic view that it gives, and the opportunities that it then affords to carry out some intelligent, and evidence-based planning for predicted needs, rather than simply reacting on an individual basis' (Cochrane, 2006).

Developing a provision map helps the school to manage different funding streams coherently to target particular patterns of need in different year groups. Priorities are established and made transparent, so that staff can see, for example, why the TA who was formerly attached to their class full-time now needs to work differently, running time-limited interventions in a number of year groups. Provision maps help schools to avoid situations where in one class there might be a teacher and three TAs, each attached to support individual children, whilst next door in a parallel class the teacher is struggling alone with no additional assistance. They also help schools to check the overall pattern of their provision, and make sure children do not become demoralised by repeating very similar interventions year after year.

Another advantage of provision maps is the basis they afford for systematic evaluation of the impact of each intervention that has been planned through the map. This gives substance to the school's SEN self-evaluation for the SEF. In relation to accountability, the provision map, combined with data on pupil outcomes, helps the school furnish the local authority with the information it needs in order to carry out its duty to monitor schools' use of SEN resources.

From the standpoint of this book an even more important advantage of provision maps is that SENCOs/INCOs and class teachers can avoid the need to write particular provisions down over and over again on a series of IEPs. Provision for individual children can be recorded by simply highlighting on a copy of the school's provision map the provision a particular child is receiving, dating the map and storing it with the child's records. This personalised map will yield good information for parents/carers and increase parental confidence that their child's needs are being comprehensively met.

Provision maps as a management tool are mainly a way of planning strategically for children with high-incidence (more common) types of additional need, and for planning the provision over which the school has control – that which it makes from its own budget, including any delegated SEN funding. For the majority of children, therefore, it will be sufficient just to highlight a standard, whole-school provision map when recording the provision made for that child.

Provision maps are also mainly about planning targeted intervention – time-limited group or one-to-one programmes used in class or on a withdrawal basis, rather than planning for general in-class support. This is because the evidence for the efficacy of such generalised support for children with the more common types of SEN is weak (Giangreco *et al.*, 1997; Blatchford *et al.*, 2002, 2004; Gerber *et al.*, 2001; Howes, 2003). Schools are in general better advised to spend their money elsewhere.

Some children, however, such as those with physical impairments or medical conditions or severe BESD, do require in-class support. So as to have all the information about the child in one place, these very individual arrangements can be recorded in the 'other' column on the provision map. The same column can be used to record the support provided by external agencies.

Keeping it simple

There is something about SEN that seems to make us manufacture complexity where none need exist. With provision maps, what started as a simple planning tool for school managers has degenerated in many local authorities into yet another bureaucratic burden. These are some examples:

- Provision maps that include Wave 1 class or subject teaching, and try to list every single adaptation that teachers make to meet particular types of SEN.
- Provision maps written individually for every child, aimed at showing exactly what is being done to meet their needs, and often running alongside IEPs.
- Provision maps which must be submitted annually to the local authority, with each provision costed, so as to 'prove' that the school has spent every penny of its delegated SEN budget.

Let us consider each of these common mistakes in turn.

It can be instructive as a one-off professional development exercise for a staff group to collate a list of teaching approaches and access strategies already used to support children with particular needs – dyslexia, for example, or autism, or language difficulties. Such an exercise enables teachers to reflect on what they are already doing well, to learn from others' ideas, and produce one collated ideas list of which they will have ownership, and therefore be more inclined to use. It will energise everyone because it follows the best principles of managing any sort of development or change – identifying what people are already doing that works, so as to do more of it in the future, more often and more systematically.

But why go to all the trouble of writing all these strategies on a provision map that is produced annually, and will become so long and complex that it loses its usefulness? Instead, the SENCO/INCO might want to develop the school's own bank of computer-held strategy sheets for each main type of SEN or disability, drawing on the ideas from the toolkit section of this book as well as those generated by staff. Once on the school's networked system, staff can quickly look up the strategy sheets when they want help in knowing how to plan differentiated learning and teaching for a child in their class.

Next, it is important to avoid turning provision maps back into another form of IEP by writing one for each individual child. This misses the point of provision mapping altogether. The questions a provision map seeks to answer are these:

? How many children have we in each year group who need additional interventions for language, literacy, mathematics, social and emotional learning and so on?
? Where do the greatest priorities for additional provision lie?
? How can we best deploy additional adult and peer support so as to meet these priorities?
? Which particular interventions will we choose to use, on the basis of their impact?
? Looking at our tracking data from last term/year, which provisions have had the desired impact, and which ought we to review?

These are very different questions from the more familiar 'What does this individual child need in the way of extra support?', which might lead a SENCO to begin by constructing a provision map for each child. That was the question to which we were led by an IEP-driven system. And an IEP-driven system led us to patterns of provision based mostly on attaching TAs as if by Velcro to individual children, to offer generalised in-class support or teaching geared around three or four IEP targets.

As we saw in Chapter 1, such a system failed to serve our children well, and failed to serve the SENCOs and teachers who drowned in paper while struggling valiantly to make it work. It is essential that provision maps do not replicate the weaknesses of the past. We need to construct them on a whole-school basis, to plan the provision in year groups, not for Saleem or Sam or Sarah. We can print and date a copy, highlighting on it the provision that Saleem receives, so as to have an ongoing child-level record on file. We can add to it the very individual arrangements, like help with toileting, and a physiotherapy programme that Sam might need. We can add to it the multi-agency support – speech and language therapy, advice from a specialist VI teacher, advice from a teacher in a local special school – that Sarah might access. We can, as we will see later in this chapter in the section on evaluation, add provision columns to the pupil-level data held in RAISEonline, and print out individual provision records. But we must start our provision planning with a proactive, strategic, whole-school focus rather than ad hoc child-by-child arrangements.

Finally, what about costing provision maps? It is not uncommon now for local authorities to require schools to produce costed maps. This is seen as helping the local authority fulfil their statutory duty of ensuring that appropriate provision is made for children with SEN, by making sure that schools are expending all their delegated SEN funding for its specified purpose.

There is not a single headteacher, however, who cannot by canny accounting demonstrate that their school is spending not only what the local authority has allocated to meet SEN in the school's budget share, but far more besides. Almost any arrangement, such as running smaller class groups or sets, providing each class with its own TA, having extra adults around to keep order at lunchtimes, having extra pastoral staff to enable a school in a difficult area to run smoothly, or buying extra computers can be allocated to a school's notional SEN budget and its provision map if the school so chooses. The definition of what constitutes SEN provision is so wide as to be meaningless. And in a sense accounting for spending is an irrelevance: what matters is the impact that the school's spending choices has on pupils. If the school chooses to spend its SEN budget on refurbishing the staffroom, and can demonstrate that the attainment and well-being of pupils with SEN or disabilities improves, then the local authority has a poor case for challenge.

Unless your school has developed a sophisticated IT system that holds data on average hourly staffing costs and does the necessary calculation, costing a provision map is a lot of work. That work should not be undertaken to fulfil someone else's purposes, if those purposes can be met in other more sensible ways. This is the case for local authorities' duty to hold schools to account for the progress of pupils with SEN or disabilities. Proffering data on pupil *outcomes* is a more sensible way of meeting that purpose.

It may be helpful to highlight or print a provision map for an individual child and cost it, if you have to give evidence at a tribunal or need to convince a parent that you are fully allocating funding granted through a Statement.

Otherwise, the only reason for costing a whole-school provision map is if doing so will meet your *own* school purpose, to raise standards and promote pupils' well-being. Here, there may be a case for costing different provisions so that you can do a cost–benefit analysis – that is, compare the costs and impact of different provisions to see which gives best value for money (the highest impact at the lowest cost). An anger-management group run by a learning mentor, for example, might prove to have an impact as great as that of one-to-one counselling from a clinical psychologist for the four individuals involved, but constitute better value for money because the unit costs of a learning mentor are very much lower than those of a clinical psychologist, and because the pupils work as a group rather than one to one.

Even here, however, schools may want to be cautious. In the example above, they would need to be sure that the pupils were comparable – that those working with the learning mentor in this case had needs just as great as those working with the clinical psychologist. One also needs to be aware that analysis that considers only *immediate* benefits and immediate costs can sometimes lead to unhelpful conclusions. Consider, for example, the Head Start programme, that provided intensive pre-school intervention for disadvantaged children. Immediate analysis showed costs to be high and the differential benefits (when compared to outcomes for similar children not involved in the programme) to be limited. It was only when the Head Start children were followed up to adulthood and found to be much less likely to have dropped out of school or to have been involved in crime, that the benefits became clear. This long-term cost-benefit analysis showed that, for every dollar spent on the programme, over $7 was saved by society.

A recent study in this country (KPMG Foundation, 2006) makes a similar point. Here, researchers compared the costs of providing the intensive, one-to-one, teacher-led, Reading Recovery programme to six-year-olds with literacy difficulties with the costs incurred by schools and society if the children's difficulties remained unaddressed. The one-off cost of offering Reading Recovery was £2,380 per child – much more expensive than an intervention delivered by a TA or delivered in a group. Yet the same six-year-old receiving less expensive but also less effective provision would cost their junior school £2,187 in special needs support over the course of Key Stage 2, and the secondary school £3,526 over the course of Key Stages 3 and 4 – over £5,500 in total. With the longer-term costs of crime, ill health and reduced employment opportunities also taken into account, the researchers estimated a return on investment of between £15 and £18 for every £1 spent on Reading Recovery.

Special educational needs that are not effectively addressed carry life-long consequences for individuals and for society. Cost–benefit analyses can be misleading if the benefits assessed are only short term, and if the analysis focuses only on the costs and benefits for the institution rather than on the wider issues of every child's right to the best possible future.

Developments in provision mapping
Extending your provision

One notable development in provision mapping in recent years has been the extension of the range of provision that is planned for. Early provision maps were often dominated by provision for pupils with literacy difficulties, with perhaps a nod to numeracy and speech and language provision. Now, a primary provision map might include four or five different literacy interventions, the Primary National Strategy Wave 3 mathematics materials, the oral language scheme *Talking Partners*, a social use of language programme and the use of social stories for children on the autistic spectrum, perhaps a motor coordination skills programme, and a range of provision for children who need extra help to develop social, emotional and behavioural skills. In the secondary school, there might be a small Year 7 nurture group for vulnerable pupils, a range of one-to-one mentoring programmes, study support, learning-to-learn courses, skilled counselling or cognitive behaviour therapy and social skills groups, as well as the usual literacy and mathematics catch-up interventions.

An important growth area is provision for pupils with BESD. The development of a 'universal' curriculum framework to teach all children social and emotional skills (the SEAL primary and secondary resources) has allowed us to apply a 'Waves' model, originally devised for literacy and numeracy, to social and emotional learning (Figure 7.2). Schools are encouraged to identify pupils who with just a little help can catch up with their peers in this area of learning, as a result of taking part in a structured group work programme, and are able to draw on a range of National Strategies materials (DfES, 2005b, 2006c; DCSF, 2007a) to help them plan, deliver and evaluate such groups. These Wave 2 developments throw into sharp focus the needs of pupils who require intervention that is much more intensive and personalised – a Wave 3 intervention delivered by a highly skilled professional, often in a multi-agency context where there is work not only with the pupil but with the family and in the community. Provision for children with attendance problems is beginning to figure on provision maps too – like the school that has organised a 'walking bus' to pick up the 20 children who were often late or attended irregularly.

Another set of opportunities for increasing the range of provision comes through the extended schools agenda. The features of an extended school (childcare, study support, parenting support, community use of facilities, access to multi-agency support) prompt us to think about how these elements can be employed to enhance the school's provision map. How, for example, can school-based literacy and numeracy intervention be enhanced by the addition of work with families such as family literacy and numeracy courses? How can school-based BESD provision be enhanced by parenting programmes, or by the involvement of the youth service in working with the pupils in their community? How can the extra *time* provided by the extended schools offer (before and after school and in the school holidays) help us overcome the problem of how to fit interventions into a crowded school day, and how to avoid pupils missing out on a broad and rich curriculum while they are having help with basic skills?

FIGURE 7.2 Waves model – behaviour/emotional health and well-being

Defining effective provision

Another development in provision mapping is the greater sense we now have of which provisions have the greatest impact on children's progress.

Research evidence for the impact of different provisions was summarised in *SEN and school improvement* (Gross and White, 2003), and updated in the National Strategies' *Leading on intervention* materials (DfES, 2006d). Since then, further research has been published and is incorporated into a summary table (Table 7.3). The table lists the interventions that schools can use with some certainty that they will have the desired effect.

Moving from provision mapping to provision management

Constructing a provision map is one thing. Making sure that the provision it describes proves effective is another. Like IEPs, provision maps run the risk of sitting in someone's drawer or on their laptop, to be pulled out when Ofsted comes but not in between.

Key to making provision maps effective are the processes which link the map to tracking information. Tracking too can become meaningless paperwork – 'fantastic folders of pupil tracking, kept in the deputy head's office but nothing done about them', as one school put it. Linking your provision map to tracking information means that the map can be regularly adjusted to meet changing needs.

Also key are the systems that are in place to monitor the quality of the provision, and to evaluate its effectiveness. The steps involved are shown in Figure 7.3.

Linking provision to performance management is a relatively new area. Although we are accustomed to linking the progress of a class or classes to teachers' performance management, and monitoring the quality of classroom and subject teaching, many schools are only just beginning to identify clearly the outcomes they expect for groups of children taking part in intervention programmes, and link these to performance management targets for the adults involved. Usually, this will be the teaching assistant who is delivering the intervention – but it is also important, in primary schools, to make similar performance management arrangements for the class teacher. This is because with an intervention it is essential that the class teacher retains overall ownership, with the TA working under his or

	PRIMARY	SECONDARY
LANGUAGE	Language development: circle time sessions to improve language skills It takes two to talk (Hanen Programme, 2–6 years) One step at a time Teaching Talking Talking Partners	
LITERACY	Acceleread, Accelewrite Better Reading Partnership Catch Up literacy Cued spelling Direct Phonics Early Literacy Support (ELS) ENABLE Family Literacy Fischer Family Trust Wave 3 Further Literacy Support Lexia Multisensory Teaching System for Reading (MTSR) Paired reading, paired writing Phono-graphix TM Reading Intervention Reading Recovery Reciprocal Teaching RML (Ruth Miskin Literacy, Read Write Inc.) SIDNEY Sound Discovery Sounds-Write Toe by Toe THRASS	Better Reading Partnership Catch Up literacy ENABLE Literacy Acceleration Paired reading Phono-graphix TM Read Write Inc.
MATHEMATICS	Family Numeracy Mathematics Recovery Numeracy Recovery Numicon Peer tutoring PNS Wave 3 mathematics	Peer tutoring
PARENTING PROGRAMMES	The Incredible Years (3–12 years) Spokes (Year 1) Triple P	Triple P The Strengthening Families Programme for Parents
SOCIAL AND EMOTIONAL LEARNING	Nurture groups, Pyramid Clubs Relaxation training Social skills groupwork such as Dinosaur School, SEAL group work, anger management Stress reduction – Place2Be, A Quiet Place Some mentoring schemes such as Chance UK Therapeutic story writing School Home Support Workers	Alternative curricula e.g. Skill Force Fairbridge Relaxation training School Home Support Workers Social skills group work such as anger management, SEAL group work Some mentoring schemes such as Chance UK and some learning support units Stress reduction

Sources and further information:
Brooks, G. (2007) *What works for children with literacy difficulties.* London: DCSF
Communities that Care (2005) *A guide to promising approaches.* London: Communities that Care
DfES (2006d) *Leading on intervention.* London: DfES
New Philanthropy Capital (2007) *Lean on me: mentoring for young people at risk.* London: NPC

TABLE 7.3 What works in intervention

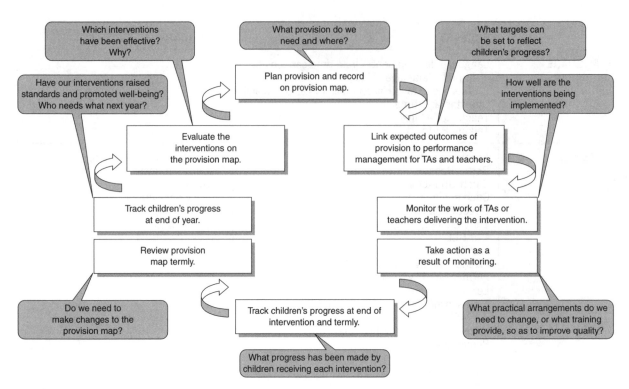

FIGURE 7.3 Provision management

her direction, with very good links made between the work the children do in the intervention programme and the work they do in class.

It is important, too, that adults delivering intervention programmes are observed from time to time. Such monitoring has several purposes. It enables a SENCO/INCO or other manager to check that the intervention is being delivered in the way intended by those who originally constructed and evaluated the programme. We know from research (Beard *et al.*, 2005) that such 'fidelity to the programme' is both highly important, in terms of programme impact, and relatively rare. Training has an immediate impact on the way we teach, but most of us are programmed to return to our default settings (the way we behaved before we had the training) over time – unless we have top-up training, observation and feedback.

Observation of interventions will also inform the professional development that should underpin any performance management cycle, and enable any practical problems to be spotted and resolved. The TA or teacher may be working in a noisy place, for example, or have children arriving in dribs and drabs to their session, without the materials they need, or opportunities for liaison between the TA and class teacher may be limited. Picking these practical issues up early will make the adult delivering the programme feel valued and enable them to make the most of the precious time they have with the children with whom they work.

The toolkit section of this book presents an exemplar framework for monitoring the quality of interventions, that allows for professional development needs to be identified and practical problems resolved.

The toolkit also includes a set of proformas ideal for use when setting up an intervention programme. The basic framework was originally developed by Sheffield local authority, and appears on the National Strategies' *Leading on intervention* CD (DfES, 2006d). Additional proformas for setting up a range of commonly used interventions are provided here; others can be developed, following the basic model, for any intervention in use at your school. The proformas support the management cycle of planning, developing, monitoring and evaluating provisions in Figure 7.3: they describe the entry criteria for the intervention, the expected outcome (exit criteria), how and when delivery will be monitored and the evaluation method that will be applied. Essentially, they enable SENCOs/INCOs to manage the school's provision for children with additional needs, once they have mapped the provision that is required.

Another time-saving tool for evaluating the school's provision comes from the use of RAISEonline. The pupil-level data function on RAISEonline allows a school to hold and import data about each of its pupils – name, gender, date of birth, SEN status, free school meals status, ethnic origin. To the basic spreadsheet a school can, with the custom attributes button, add further columns, one for each provision on the school's provision map. Putting a 'Y' in the relevant columns allows for a personalised printout of the provision received by each child, if you want to use this as an alternative to highlighting a paper version of your whole-school provision map.

More importantly, however, recording each child's provision on a database enables you to evaluate the impact of your provisions. You can, for example, using the filtering function pull out only those pupils who have received a particular intervention, such as anger-management groups, and print out their exclusion data, attendance data, end of key stage test results and results of any additional assessments (such as QCA optional tests or reading ages) that have been entered onto RAISEonline. You can refine your evaluation by, for example, pulling out only boys who have had a particular provision, or only girls, or only those in a certain year group, or with a particular type of SEN. Such sophisticated applications of data represent a powerful tool for evaluating a provision map, and promise much for the future in terms of reducing the workload involved in proper evaluation.

Working in Partnership
Parents, Pupils and Outside Agencies

Working with parents and carers

Working effectively with parents and carers is the key to reducing bureaucracy. If parents are confident about what is being done to support their child, they do not need pieces of paper. They can be your greatest ally in reducing bureaucracy, or – if you get the relationship with them wrong – they can undo all your efforts. Not least, they can exercise their legal right to request a statutory assessment for a possible Statement of SEN that will generate a blizzard of paperwork for you and the local authority.

So it is essential that, in making any changes to the way you manage SEN and disability in school, you do this with the full support of parents and carers.

Systems for involving parents/carers

Ideally, you will begin by finding out, perhaps through a questionnaire or focus-group discussion, how parents/carers feel about your current procedures. They may be happy – but they may not. Research shows that parental involvement remains a real challenge for schools. Rathbone (2001), for example, found that nearly half of parents surveyed did not feel involved in reviews of the child's progress and, while the majority believed that they could contribute vital information about their child's needs, schools did not always seek out or use this information. Jones and Swain (2001) similarly report a picture of parents feeling defeated by bureaucracy. Pinkus (2005) researched the experiences of 14 parents in four local authorities as they 'worked in partnership with professionals to meet the needs of their SEN children', and found that parents often felt that they only attended meetings to listen to what professionals had to say. Their perception was that decisions had already been made, for example, when they were asked to sign IEPs that had been written before the meeting started. Many parents find the paperwork involved in SEN full of jargon, and are aware that some of the child's teachers may not even read it, particularly when the child changes class or school. Significantly, what they want and do not always feel they get is information on what they can do to help their child with learning.

If your own research shows that parents and carers have concerns about current systems, you will find it easy to explain why you are making changes, such as no longer having IEPs for all children with SEN. You might want to invite parents to a meeting to explain any changes; you will certainly want to supply all of them with information in leaflet form. The toolkit section of this book presents a possible model for you to build on.

You will want to make clear the advantages of the new approach – for example, the expectation that class or subject teachers build a knowledge of the child's individual needs into their everyday planning. Parents/carers will also be very interested to see the school's provision map, with entry and exit criteria for each additional intervention, so that they know what provision they can expect for their child.

It is very important to find out, too, about any worries your parents/carers may have. These will be particular to your setting but might be about having less contact with you as the SENCO/INCO, if meetings to review progress are more often to be led by the class teacher or form tutor. You will need to be clear what arrangements there will be for others (such as you, or a head of year, or the child's key worker in school) to routinely join review meetings involving pupils with SEN or behaviour difficulties. You could also make clear that there will be no change to the kind of informal communication lines (telephone contact, drop-in times and so on) that parents/carers generally value far more than the more formal channels.

Parents/carers will want to know not just what you are stopping doing, but also what you are planning to do instead. It will be helpful to explain your plans for:

- involving them, as the experts on their own child, in providing information and feedback to the school;
- making sure all relevant staff are aware of their child's needs;
- setting targets;
- reviewing and reporting on progress;
- making additional provision for the child;
- generating ideas on how they can help their child at home.

In other chapters we have seen how these areas can be addressed in non-bureaucratic ways. Parents can be given a highlighted provision map so that they know exactly what provision their child receives. They can furnish information about their child through a discussion based on the five Every Child Matters outcomes, and contribute to the pupil-held Personal Profiles like those described in the case studies in Chapter 2. They should have sent home to them every term the (differentiated) targets that their child will be working on in class, or see these recorded in the child's Learning Log or planner.

Ideally, the targets for all children in the class will be linked to information on how the family can help the child achieve them. Some schools, for example, post on the web the learning programmes for the week, with some suggestions about how parents/carers can help at home. Others put a poster on a door or window where parents bringing or collecting their children will see it. Really useful materials for home activities are available from the National Strategies on the Standards Site, in the form of leaflets for parents of primary children (DfES, 2004f) and web-based printable guidance for parents of secondary-aged children (DfES, 2006e). An example is shown in Table 8.1.

Parents'/carers' involvement in reviews of progress might, for some children with more complex SEN, take the form of specially convened meetings. But for many children they will take place at regular parents' evenings – perhaps with more time allocated to the meeting than might be standard for other pupils. Or they may take place at special academic tutoring days, like those at Coombe Boys' School in the case study in Chapter 2, where

YEAR 2 READING: STORIES	Home activities
I can use a contents list and index and tell a friend what a book might be about by looking at the cover, title and illustrations.	Use a TV listings guide to choose programmes that you would like to watch together.

YEAR 2 MATHEMATICS: MEASURING	Home activities
I can estimate the lengths of different objects, compare their size and measure them, and compare their length.	Have your child stand in a doorway in your house. Say that the doorway is roughly 2 metres high. Ask your children how many things they can see that are taller/shorter than 2 metres.

TABLE 8.1 Taking an active interest in your child's learning

parents, pupil and form tutor meet together on an appointment basis, joined where necessary by specialist colleagues.

In between reviews, the most effective schools employ a range of strategies, including the internet, to keep parents/carers in touch with how their child is doing. Cardinal Wiseman Secondary School in Birmingham, for example, allows parents/carers password-protected access to regularly updated information on their child's academic progress, conduct log and attendance record. All pupils have targets that are reviewed termly; progress against these targets is regularly tracked and assessment information placed on the e-portal. Some 65 per cent of parents at the school have internet access, even though it serves an area of high social deprivation (46 per cent free school meals). Parents who do not have internet access receive printed versions of assessment information, and pupils also put their targets (on sticky labels) in their homework diaries.

ICT is also put to good effect at Eggbuckland College in Plymouth. Here, pupils all have an electronic individual learning plan. The e-ILP can be added to by pupils and teachers, and can hold anything from targets to action plans to personal blogs. It forms the basis for the school's twice-yearly review days, when parents come into school for three-way meetings with their child and the form tutor.

South Dartmoor College in Devon operates a similar system of personalised appointments. The college allocates a day a week each February for these reviews. Much effort goes into making sure parents/carers make and keep appointments; where necessary they are reminded by phone or an EWO visit. As a result, attendance at the review days has risen from 70 per cent to almost 100 per cent. Parents/carers of KS4 pupils have subject-specific meetings, but in KS3 the meeting is with the form tutor. The school uses SIMS Parents' Gateway to produce information on progress in all subjects; the tutor and parents can call up the data on screen and discuss it together.

The government plans that all schools will by 2010 have a 'learning platform' with personal access and information for each pupil. When this happens, it will become even easier for more schools to operate electronic systems like those employed at South Dartmoor and Eggbuckland. Learning platforms allow parents to see their children's marks and assignments, records of behaviour and attendance, and a range of other information about what the child is studying. One can easily imagine that this is where the targets and other information that would once have been on an IEP will

139

be held in future, with the child's school-based 'learning guide' or personal tutor updating the information at regular intervals.

Helping parents/carers to help their child – whole-school approaches

As we have seen, the biggest gap for parents/carers in our current SEN procedures is their failure to support them in knowing how best to help their child in the areas where they are experiencing difficulty. Equally, we know how fundamental it is for the child's progress that there is home support for learning. Recent influential research (Desforges and Abouchaar, 2003) has shown that, where parents/carers are involved, on average children's attainment will be 15–17 per cent higher than where they are not involved.

The type of involvement that brings these gains is not about 'coming into school' – attending school events, turning up at parents' evenings, helping in class and so on. What makes the difference instead is what Desforges and Abouchaar calls good at-home parenting. This entails the provision of 'a secure and stable environment, intellectual stimulation, parent–child discussion, good models of constructive social and educational values and high aspirations relating to personal fulfilment and good citizenship'. A key element of this is the quality of the 'home learning environment' (Sylva *et al.*, 2003): the extent to which parents/carers talk to and play with their child, take them on outings, read to them, teach nursery rhymes and songs, play with numbers and letters and so on. And this is not dependent on the social class or educational level of parents and carers; as Sylva says, 'What you do is more important than who you are.'

How can we help all families practise this sort of good at-home parenting? It is clear that the SENCO/INCO cannot achieve this by working on their own. Involving parents/carers of children with SEN or disabilities, or of EAL learners or other vulnerable groups, needs to build on an existing ethos which conveys to parents/carers that they are valued partners rather than potential trouble-makers.

An ethos like this is often tangibly conveyed in some schools, whilst absent in others. It can be conveyed, for example, by the school entrance hall, where local radio might be playing (rather than Mozart), where the reading matter on the table in the comfortable waiting area includes *Hello* magazine as well as the school prospectus. There could be information in community languages, and posters inviting parents to join in various activities, some of which are deliberately unthreatening to a parent whose own experience of learning may hitherto have been negative – everything from nail art, stress workshops, massage, art and craft and ICT through to the more 'academic' curriculum workshops and Family Learning courses.

Care will be taken that parents' and carers' first communication with school are not about any difficulties their child may have. A relationship will have been built up long before this, which focuses on sharing information about the child as a person and a learner (not a 'special needs child'), and which celebrates strengths and successes, for example, by sending home 'praise postcards' to let parents know when things have gone well.

In these schools special efforts will be made to reach out to fathers. Fathers' involvement in their child's learning is strongly related to educational attainment and adjustment, particularly for boys (Flouri and Buchanan, 2002). In the teenage years, one study showed that 90 per cent of boys who felt that their father spent time with them and took an active interest in their progress were confident and successful. By contrast, 72 per cent of those who said their fathers rarely or never did these things fell into the group with the lowest levels of self-confidence, and were more likely to dislike school and get in trouble with the police.

The case studies below give examples of the kind of imaginative work schools have done to engage parents in children's learning. They represent the type of practice the SENCO/INCO, as part of the school leadership team, will want to develop in their school.

CASE STUDY

Birley Spa Primary in Sheffield used the Index for Inclusion (CSIE, 2002) to undertake a self-evaluation of inclusive cultures, policy and practice. As part of this review they surveyed parents, and employed the information gained to re-shape aspects of the way they work with the community. Parents were involved in working groups to tackle issues such as communication. A support group was set up for parents who might have concerns, for example, about bullying, but did not initially feel confident to talk to staff. Every day there are as many as 80 parents and carers in the school, lending volunteer support in classrooms, attending courses as adult learners, or helping with childcare for the many adult education courses available. These cover subjects requested by local people, such as ICT. Adults who take part in these courses are supported to progress, where they want to, to obtain qualifications at the local college.

CASE STUDY

At Arbourthorne Primary, also in Sheffield, a concerted drive to improve the relationship between the school and parents led to the appointment of key staff to lead the work – a deputy head and a learning mentor, who spent time chatting to parents, inviting them in for coffee, and going into the playground every day to invite reluctant parents in to watch a lesson. Children and families were given special interactive homework that involved them in working together; this project was given high status, with parents actively involved in generating feedback and helping shape future work. The school arranged opportunities for parents and children to work together in school with visiting artists, and organised a range of courses in and out of school including ICT, book keeping, and Basic Skills literacy. After two years the school had established a group of parents who by now were very comfortable in school and in supporting their children's learning. These parents now organise themselves and decided on the next steps, which have included setting up a very successful credit union, running a fruit snack shop in school, the establishment of a PTA and regular curriculum workshops where teachers explain what children will be learning, what homework will be involved, and how parents can help.

CASE STUDY

Cooper's Lane Primary School in Lewisham devised a 'Dads Matter' scheme. A group of fathers and male family figures have been meeting once a month in a local pub or restaurant to plan a strategy to encourage fathers to become more involved with their children's learning. Support is particularly targeted at families of children with behaviour difficulties, because few of them have experienced positive male role models. The group planned trips, home reading activities, fun homework tasks and a 'Bring your dad to school day', when dads would come in and use their talents and interests to work with children. One father, for example, brought in his motorbike to show to the boys. About 60 fathers took part in the first year of the scheme, which had a marked impact. Fathers became much more confident to come into the playground and into school, and there has been a reduction in behaviour problems amongst the target children.

Where schools set up initiatives like these they are establishing the essential backdrop against which the SENCO or INCO can build their own targeted work with families of children who have SEN or disabilities.

This backdrop is particularly important where children have behavioural, emotional and social difficulties. Research shows that support for their parents in developing their parenting skills can have a huge impact (National Institute for Health and Clinical Excellence, 2006). But the parenting programmes that work, such as those described in Chapter 7, can easily feel stigmatising and uncomfortable for parents/carers. Very few schools succeed by simply inviting targeted parents to attend a parenting course. The potential stigma around such courses, and a general feeling amongst most parents that they should somehow automatically know how to bring up a child, act as a powerful deterrent. Schools have to work hard to overcome these barriers. Where they are successful, it is usually because they have built up 'parental capital' by offering parents a range of non-threatening and enjoyable activities. These, as we have seen, help create the climate where parenting skills courses can be offered as a natural progression for parents/carers who are already confident in coming into school. After that, a good way in is to offer SEAL Family Learning workshops (DfES, 2006b) to *all* parents/carers in a non-stigmatising way, then follow this up with more intensive work with some.

Helping parents/carers of children with SEN or disabilities to help their child

The extended schools agenda is involving more and more schools in whole-school effort to involve parents/carers. Given this backdrop, what more can be done to support parents/carers of children with SEN or disabilities?

Overcoming barriers

First, SENCOs/INCOs will need to make special efforts to draw some of these parents into what the school has to offer. Many experience particular barriers to involvement. Their own experience of education may make them anxious or angry when coming into school or talking to teachers. They may themselves have poor literacy or numeracy skills which make it difficult for them to help their child. Their feelings about their child's difficulties are often those that cause awkwardness in their relationship with the school. They may simply get tired of hearing yet another teacher telling them that their child has problems.

But as Klein (2000) puts it, 'Parents don't exist solely as the receptacles of bad news about their children's problem behaviour or poor attainment.' The best SENCOs/INCOs understand this and go out of their way to overcome barriers and provide extra nurturing for parents as well as pupils. At Coombe Boys', the case study school in Chapter 2, the SENCO put time and energy into making that all-important first contact with parents/carers. If they would not come to school, she would visit them at home, together with an education welfare officer. In the first meeting she would highlight specific positives about their child, and introduce them personally to a person in school (one of the TA team, for example) whom they could contact at any time. After the first meeting she would nurture the relationship by being available in person or on the phone when parents needed to talk, by checking with them when any changes were proposed to the child's pattern of support, and by offering practical help. All parents of children with SEN or disabilities in Year 7 were invited to a coffee morning at the start of the school year. There, they heard about the school support systems and could chat informally with the school's educational psychologist, transition worker, head of year and SENCO. Through measures like these, Coombe was able to achieve 100 per cent parental attendance at review meetings.

A primary school in Bristol, serving one of the most deprived areas of the city, achieves 95 per cent attendance at parents' evenings. The school day starts early and finishes late – with breakfast clubs and after-school clubs covering family literacy, numeracy and mother tongue classes where parents learn alongside their children. There are also sewing, art, gardening and health classes and every subject coordinator runs sessions explaining how their subject is taught. Families take part in maths trails, drama workshops, musical sessions and various environmental and geographical trails. Drop-in sessions are available for parents with pre-school children and there are pre-nursery home visits for all. Parents are always welcome in school, helping in classes and sitting on working groups. They work with the children on computers, with art activities, literacy-based lessons and in after-hours clubs.

Parents' evenings are where initial discussion about a child with SEN takes place and, if parents do not attend, then someone in school will try to catch them later: 'We missed you at parents' evening – how about popping in tomorrow after school?' Teachers stress the positives: 'He did a fantastic piece of work on robots. Why don't you come in and see his books – you'll be pleased.' Class teachers have an informal chat to parents before any sort of formal letter about SEN goes home, and the SENCO follows up with another chat. The school will always telephone a parent who is known to have literacy difficulties, rather than write to them. The SENCO has set up a support group for parents of children with SEN or disabilities. The group meets once a week for coffee; parents might watch a video on how to help their child at home, borrow reading books or make a game to play with their child.

Practice of this kind challenges our assumptions that some parents will never be able to become involved or support their child's learning. Other ideas for engaging parents of children with SEN or disabilities include:

- inviting a group of parents whose children have the same type of SEN, or are in the same year group, to get together on a one-off or regular basis;
- having a drop-in 'surgery' session at a fixed time each week that is convenient for parents;
- using email, voice and text messages to remind parents of review meetings or send 'good news' home;
- pairing a parent or family with another in a buddying relationship – someone you can always ring up, for example, if the child has forgotten what the homework was meant to be;
- running a link parent scheme, where a group of parents whose children have transferred to a secondary school continue to attend activities for Year 6 parents so as to support the family over the transition;
- having a room or space specifically for parents of children with SEN or disabilities, with information leaflets, videos and access to helpful websites.

Involving parents in interventions

Having built bridges and forged relationships, the next step for the SENCO/INCO – and one which applies equally to parents/carers who are keen to come into school and knowledgeable about their rights – is to have systems that afford clear information about the provision available in school, and involve the parent/carer in decisions to implement a particular intervention or to review its impact. This is where the provision map is such a helpful tool, particularly if it is combined with clear information about the entry and exit criteria for each provision.

Wherever possible, each intervention should have parental involvement built into its design. Examples of this are:

- the 'take-homes' in Early Literacy Support (ELS);
- the ideas for home activities in the primary strategy 'Supporting pupils with gaps in their mathematical understanding' materials;
- the Incredible Years parent programme that runs parallel to the Dino Dinosaur social skills group work for four to eight year olds.

The provision planning proformas in the toolkit section of this book signpost the importance of parental engagement within each intervention; if you are developing a planning proforma for an intervention of your own, it will be useful to think about and record this element.

Some interventions ask parents/carers to sign up to a semi-formal contract that sets out what the school will deliver, and what the parent is asked to do in return. The well-known Reading Recovery literacy intervention, for example, relies on the child being in school daily for their 12–20 week series of lessons. Where children have attendance problems, there will be a chat with the parents about the investment that the school is making in the child for this very intensive and expensive intervention, and the effects if the child misses sessions. The message is 'If you can get your child to school we will make sure they get their daily lesson and they will learn to read really well.' Parents are invited to watch a lesson and the teacher will spend time with them afterwards discussing what they saw. Parents also sign up to work with their child every day on the Reading Recovery 'homework'. This is carefully planned so that it does not ask parents/carers to do anything that might cause difficulty. They simply hear their child read one or more short books that the child can already tackle well independently, and help the child reconstruct a cut-up sentence that they have written and already reassembled and re-read several times in their lesson in school.

Workshops and courses

Finally, the SENCO/INCO will want to build on the provision the child receives in school with linked, targeted workshops or courses which will model for the parent the ways in which they can help the child at home. Although IEPs were meant to guide parents on how to help, they do not – according to parents – seem to have succeeded. Often the ideas written on them are too general: 'Hear Jack read every day' can leave the parent wondering how exactly they should do this. What is more helpful is a practical demonstration. An example for literacy might be a paired reading workshop for a group of parents in which they learn how to follow a very simple procedure – first the parent and child read simultaneously out loud until the child signals (for example, by knocking on the table) that he wants to read by himself, then the child reads independently until they get stuck or make a mistake, when the parent joins in until the child signals again, and so on. Another alternative is to train parents as Better Reading Partners, adapting the scheme developed by Bradford local authority.

A wide range of possible courses – workshops that feature practical demonstration – is available. Table 8.2 shows some of the activities that could be offered, many of them by local authority Family Learning services. The SENCO/INCO's role is to bring together a group of parents whose children have similar provision in school, for shared sessions where they can both learn new techniques to help their child, and also lend each other with mutual support. Often the sessions include 'take-home' elements; for

SPECIAL EDUCATIONAL NEED	COURSES FOR PARENTS/CARERS
Literacy	Paired reading workshops. SHARE: workshops for small groups of parents that provide ideas and resources for learning activities to share with their children at home. INSPIRE: a Birmingham programme to encourage parents to be involved in developing their children's literacy skills. Family literacy: aims to raise standards of literacy for both parents and children. Keeping up with the children: introduces parents to the way their children are taught literacy in school, so that they can be confident in supporting them. Spokes parenting programme: a programme aimed mainly at improving behaviour in Y1 children, but also helps parents support their children's literacy development.
Language	Locally run Family Learning programmes such as Family Talk.
Mathematics	SHARE: workshops for small groups of parents that provide ideas and resources for learning activities to share with their children at home. INSPIRE: a Birmingham programme to encourage parents to be involved in developing their children's numeracy skills. Keeping up with the children: introduces parents to the way their children are taught mathematics in school, so that they can be confident in supporting them. Family numeracy: aims to raise standards of numeracy for both parents and children.
Social and emotional skills	Family SEAL. Parenting skills courses such as Incredible Years, Triple P, Mellow Parenting, Positive Parents, Spokes.

TABLE 8.2 Courses and workshops for families

example, some schools have developed paired maths schemes, with a stock of games coded according to the maths skill or concept involved and with an accompanying card to highlight the kinds of mathematical language the game could bring out. Parents borrow a game or two each week, and record how play went in a home-school book.

Such workshops and courses can be really successful with lower-attaining pupils. Evaluations of Family Literacy and Numeracy courses for parents of three to six year olds, for example (Brooks, 1996, 1998), showed that the proportion of children whose low reading level would leave them struggling in school fell from 67 per cent to 9 per cent, and the proportion whose even lower reading level would leave them severely disadvantaged for learning fell from 24 per cent to 9 per cent. Progress in number and mathematical language was also good. Equally, parenting skills courses can halve the rate of severe behaviour problems (Scott *et al.*, 2001), with improvements maintained up to ten years later (NICE, 2006).

Another idea is to invite a parent in to work with their child and a teaching assistant in school once a week, or to have a TA or family support/home school worker implement a time-limited home visiting programme. For young children with significant learning difficulties, the Portage scheme represents an outstandingly successful model. Here, a specially trained Portage worker visits the home once a week to model for the parent the games and activities that will help the child achieve specific next steps in their learning – whether it be language and communication, motor skills, or cognitive development. A home visiting scheme has also been used for early literacy skills; one small-scale research study (Feiler, 2003) sent a TA to visit parents of reception children once a week for about an hour, and showed that the children supported caught up with their peers by the end of the year.

Involving pupils

Pupil involvement is flagged up as a fundamental element of effective SEN practice in the SEN Code and accompanying toolkit (DfES, 2001a). Yet, two years after the revised Code and all the training that accompanied it, Norwich and Kelley (2004), in a survey of over 400 SENCOs, found extreme variance in school practice. There has been a great deal of excellent work done since then on how to seek the views of children and young people with learning and communication difficulties, how to prepare pupils with more complex needs to take an active part in annual Statement reviews and Transition reviews. Yet the involvement of pupils with high-incidence types of SEN remains tokenistic. The volume of IEPs which schools have tried to manage has meant that they have become formulaic – a piece of paper rather than a record of dialogue and joint planning involving pupil, parent/carer and the school. As such, pupils are often not involved at all or, if they are, the involvement may constitute of no more than putting their signature to targets that the adults have already dictated, and reports of progress in which they have had little or no say.

What, then, can the alternative SEN systems suggested in this book, based on intensifying for some pupils the whole-school systems for personalising learning applied to all pupils, offer in terms of pupil involvement?

The benefits are significant, not least because they are based on a cultural shift we are seeing in many schools, following the insights gleaned from Assessment for Learning theorists and practitioners. Assessment for Learning, as we saw in Chapter 4, encourages teachers to help children take responsibility for their own learning, playing a part in assessing their own progress and deciding what they need to learn next. In some schools, pupils actually *lead* reviews with their parents and tutors, contributing their own views on how they are doing before asking others to comment. All this is a far cry from educational models of learners as passive receptacles of subject knowledge imparted by adults, that held sway in many secondary schools in the past.

The changing culture in schools, then, forms the backdrop for improved participation for pupils with SEN or disabilities. And the case studies in Chapter 2 show how schools can build on this backdrop, by involving pupils in setting their own targets (some personal, some academic), in taking part in regular review meetings held at parents' evenings or academic mentoring days, in contributing to a Personal Profile that can inform staff about what their particular needs are and which forms of support they find helpful.

All this will not happen, however, without specific help from SENCOs/INCOs. Pupils who have for so long had the label 'SEN' applied to them by others, rather than being asked how they want to be identified and discussed, are not necessarily ready to hold their own profiles or tell adults what they need in the way of help. A legacy of shame and stigma lies between the children we are now identifying as 'special needs pupils' and those of the future, who may be part of a culture where all pupils are encouraged to identify their strengths and weaknesses, and understand that they may all need a little extra help from time to time. The intensification of 'normal' systems used for all pupils is one way of achieving this kind of culture. Another is work with all pupils, and with staff, to promote disability awareness and disability equality, and on the effects of stigma, teasing and name-calling. This can be followed up by specific mentoring of individual pupils by disabled older peers and adults – to help them define themselves confidently as disabled and articulate equally confidently what they need and don't need from those around them. SENCOS/INCOs' involvement in training pupils in self-advocacy, and creating a climate where pupils can ask for what they need as of right, is vital in beating bureaucracy. In the end, those who are best positioned to make sure their needs are met are pupils themselves. It is the pupils themselves who are always there, in every teaching and learning situation, with every supply teacher for the class, in every part of the extended school's day. If we can help them communicate their needs, many of the elaborate and paper-driven SEN systems that we have designed to fulfil this communication role may become redundant.

Involving outside agencies

Some of the bureaucracy in SEN is about trying to protect the interests of pupils and parents. As we have seen so far in this chapter, there may be more effective ways of achieving this than bits of paper that surface from time to time and are then forgotten.

Another function of bureaucracy, however, is one of gate-keeping and rationing limited resources. Psychology services, learning and behaviour support services, speech and language therapists and social services resort to paperwork to try and manage an open-ended demand for services that they are simply not staffed to meet.

Quite rightly, these agencies have to ration what they provide, for example by offering services only where the school itself can demonstrate that it has made substantial efforts to understand and help the child from its own resources, before asking for outside help. The result is often a set of complex referral forms, a different one for each agency, accompanied by requests for copies of recent IEPs. Quite rightly, too, external agencies require information in order to gain a good picture of a child's profile and needs, and what has been tried so far to help them. On this they can build their own interventions.

SENCOs and INCOs are not in control of the systems adopted by outside agencies. They can, however, seek to influence them. Increasingly, the Every Child Matters (ECM) agenda is meaning that a group of professionals work in a locality with a defined group of schools. There is often an opportunity for headteachers and SENCOs/INCOs to sit on local management groups or panels that help to develop the local systems responsible for allocating time and managing referrals.

One helpful development from the ECM agenda that SENCOs/INCOs can seek to bring about in their own area avoids referral forms altogether by having regular in-school multi-agency meetings. These can take various forms. They may be formal and infrequent, like the ones described in the case studies in Chapter 2. Or they may be smaller and more frequent – for example, involving a monthly hour with the school's educational psychologist (EP), EWO and school nurse, at which actions for previous meetings are reviewed and four or five children or families discussed in depth. Other agencies can be invited when their presence will be relevant to a particular child to be discussed.

If it is not possible to influence outside agencies' referral systems so that referrals stem from face-to-face contact rather than forms in triplicate, SENCOs/INCOs should try to insist that just one multi-purpose form is used by all agencies. They can also circumvent the form by copying existing paperwork that they hold on the child, rather than starting afresh. They might, for example, copy:

- the latest pupil Personal Profile;
- a highlighted provision map showing the support the child receives;
- recent tracking data.

The only thing that they might need to add to this is a very clear description of what they want from the agency. Is it assessment to help clarify needs? Is it training for those working with the child in school? Is it direct therapeutic input that no one in the school has the skills (or could acquire the skills through training) to deliver? Is it support for the family? Is it simply extra resources?

Schools will also have to fall in, no doubt, with the requirements of the Common Assessment Form (CAF) and a shared database on children, both key elements in the government ECM agenda and drive to promote information sharing and communication between agencies. It remains to be seen whether the bureaucracy involved proves over the top in relation to the benefits it brings. It may be that it will achieve its aim of making sure that no child falls through the net, but equally we should not be surprised if overstretched and fallible human beings still fail to communicate, despite a form and database to help them do so. Meanwhile, a suggestion to SENCOs/INCOs might be that they avoid being seduced by an elegantly designed CAF into spending hours and hours inputting information that no one else will really look at. As ever, it would be wise to be clear with local colleagues what the school's information is needed for – the purpose behind the request – and seek ways of meeting the purposes rather than necessarily the bureaucracy around them.

9 | **Making the Change**

It will be clear by now to those reading this book that its theme is not only a reduction in bureaucracy, but also a fundamental rethink of the way we manage SEN and disability in schools.

This kind of rethink will involve a lot of people in school changing the way they do things. It will not be enough for the SENCO/INCO to announce to colleagues that in future there will be fewer IEPs and fewer Statements, and that they will be expected to take more responsibility for the targets, progress monitoring and strategies adopted to support pupils with SEN. Change, alas, is not that easy. As Everard and Morris (1990) say:

> implementing change is not a question of defining an end and letting others get on with it: it is a process of interaction, dialogue, feedback, modifying objectives, recycling plans, coping with mixed feelings and values, pragmatism, frustration, patience and muddle.

This chapter suggests a process a school might want to deploy to manage the change and overcome some of the difficulties inherent in any alteration in 'the way we do things here'. It is based on the work of theorists like Michael Fullan (2001) and presented as a series of principles which could help to develop your own plan for change in school.

RECOMMENDED PROCESS

Managing change

1 The change process works best when it offers a change that meets people's needs, offering them a chance of solving a problem for them or the institution.
2 The process of change must be owned by and negotiated with those involved in it.
3 Those managing the change should try to involve as many people as possible, but make sure that they involve people who have power.

4 Those managing the change must consider who else has the power to block the proposed change.

5 Those managing the change must consider what resources will realistically be needed for the new system to work, and make sure that these are built into the school development plan.

6 Effective change requires a blend of pressure and support.

7 In the implementation phase of any change, people need continued repetition of what will happen, reminders through several channels, and patient explanation of the details.

8 Once a change has been implemented, it needs to be 'institutionalised' or embedded.

Meeting needs

The first principle of successful change is that the people involved see it as necessary, linked to needs in their institution rather than imposed arbitrarily from outside. In relation to beating bureaucracy, this might mean that you need to begin by investigating, as part of your school self-evaluation, how stakeholders (staff, pupils, parents, you as coordinator) really feel about your current SEN systems. It might also mean collecting evidence about the impact of your current systems. Are pupils with SEN or disabilities doing well in your school? What do the data show? What national data might you present to staff about, for example, the impact that prevailing bureaucratic models of meeting SEN have actually had on children's progress? Chapter 1 will help you here.

This kind of self-evaluation will allow you to demonstrate to stakeholders that there really is a problem – one that they have helped to identify.

Owning the change

People will adopt new systems with energy and commitment if they have had a say in creating them. Once you have presented relevant information from your self-evaluation (which will almost always show that people are spending a lot of time on paperwork that isn't felt to benefit children), you will need a way of involving stakeholders in coming up with alternative systems to meet the functions we identified in Chapter 3:

- identification;
- assessment;
- communication;
- identifying priorities and setting targets for learning or behaviour;
- planning strategies, in the classroom and elsewhere, to help the child achieve targets;
- reviewing progress and celebrating success;
- engaging parents and carers;
- coordinating the actions to be taken by the school and outside agencies;
- informing decisions about the allocation of resources;
- supporting transition.

You might want to do this by setting up a small working group, with representation from parents, pupils and staff. Or you might want to ask for time at a primary staff meeting, or secondary faculty meetings, and with a focus group of parents, to ask for people's ideas.

Involving those with power

Successful change is not possible in any institution if the people in positions of power or influence are not behind it. This means of course that you can do nothing without first seeking the support of the headteacher and other senior managers. Your self-evaluation information will be powerful here, but there may be anxieties or resistance – perhaps a worry that parents will be upset and complain if they no longer have the apparent security of an IEP, or perhaps a wish to maintain the status quo because the current bureaucratic systems meet the local authority's needs and secure additional resources for the school (through Statements, for example). You need to identify in advance what these concerns or issues might be, and plan the reassurances that you will give – about how you are taking parents with you in moving to a new system, for example, or how changes in the local authority resourcing system mean that the drive for Statements is no longer as relevant.

Power to block

Everard and Morris (1990) divide those involved in change into four groups:

1 those who are ready to oppose the change;
2 those who are willing to let it happen;

3 those who are willing to help it happen;

4 those who are willing to make it happen.

This means making sure that you enlist those who you think will really want the change to happen as allies from the start – for example, key members of each subject department in a secondary school, or key parents who have influence on others. It also means that you need to think carefully about who might be worried about your new ideas, how you can respond to their worries, and how you can make sure you involve them actively in the planning. The chart in Table 9.1 below may help.

Building in resources

Successful change is often demanded but rarely achieved without the provision of at least some additional resources. In relation to new SEN systems, it will be helpful to ask staff, at the stage when you are working together to agree the new system, to identify the resources necessary to make the change work. The resources identified will most likely be time, for staff INSET and for them to take a new look at differentiation within their medium- and short-term planning. Time will also be needed for you to work alongside them to support improved practice.

These are some ways in which schools have created time:

- In one school, the head instituted a curriculum day when she brought in a team from outside the school to work with the children on creative projects. This freed up staff to work in phase teams on differentiated planning.
- In another school, twice-termly staff meetings are set aside for phase-based curriculum planning.
- Another school established a buddy system for planning. Foundation Stage and KS1 teachers were paired with KS2 teachers, so that they could help them plan work for older children working significantly below age-related expectations.
- Another school reduced the SENCO/INCO's teaching load for one year, so as to free him to work with subject colleagues in a cycle that involved joint planning, teaching and review.

CONCERN	POSSIBLE STRATEGIES
Class teachers: • The more children I have with IEPs, the more TA support I will get in my class. • Doing all this brings more resources through external agencies and Statements. • It will mean more work for me.	• Show how the audit of needs and provision map provides the fairest match of resources to need. • Point out the changed Statementing policies and the ways you can now access local multi-agency support teams. • Offer to work alongside the teacher to help with planning and target setting. • Show how time will be provided to support this. • Work in stages; try out the new system with just one willing year group or faculty, for example, and get them to report back.
Parents: • The teachers won't know my child has SEN. • My child won't get the help they need. • I won't know what is happening for my child and how they are doing. • I won't be involved in helping my child at home.	• Involve parents and pupils in devising a format for a Personal Profile for pupils with additional needs. • Show how the provision map works. • Show examples of differentiated classroom planning. • Ask parents to comment on your planned systems and formats for tracking and monitoring progress. • Provide information on surgeries, drop-in times, and review meetings. • Supply information on the workshops and courses provided in school.
SENCO/INCO: • Without the security of IEPs, I won't have a handle any more on what is happening, and staff won't use strategies/make an effort to meet SEN.	• I can monitor what is happening by looking at plans and through classroom observation and talking to pupils.
All: • It may not work.	• Build in an abort button – we will try the new system till x and then review it – if we aren't happy we can go back to the old system.

TABLE 9.1 Strategies to address concerns

Pressure and support

Good ideas are not enough on their own. If change is to happen, people need both ongoing support and also in some cases an element of pressure. Pressure, as discussed in Chapter 6, can be exerted through the school's regular performance management systems – through targets set for all staff, and outcomes monitored not just by the SENCO/INCO but by other senior managers. Support, as we have seen, can take many forms – INSET, buddying, opportunities for staff to observe each other's teaching, scope to look at the targets set for pupils across different classes and subjects, and chances to work alongside the SENCO/INCO or with outside agencies.

Effective support means not expecting staff to become experts in personalisation overnight. The ideas in this book ask a lot of them. They will need to plan for a range of learning objectives in one class, adopt access strategies and varied, inclusive teaching approaches, and help pupils set and review both academic and personal targets. It will work best if you start small, perhaps getting to grips with tracking backwards and forwards in objectives frameworks to identify appropriate learning objectives before asking staff to think about access strategies. And the SENCO/INCO can help staff apply simple systems to help themselves change their practice, as in this example:

> One SENCO suggested to colleagues that they identify two or three inclusive teaching strategies for lower-attaining children, and for their highest attainers, that they wanted to use more often. They then put these up on post-its on the wall, so as to remind themselves throughout the day. 'Make it personal' (i.e. link an explanation to pupils' own real-life experience), 'Chunk my instructions', 'Teach the key vocabulary I'm using' were examples of strategies staff chose for themselves. They also decided that to stretch higher attainers they wanted to ask more higher-order questions using words like 'deduce', 'predict', 'infer', so put these up on post-its too and set themselves a target of asking at least one or two in each session.

Updates during implementation

Telling people once about a change is not enough. The SENCO/INCO will need to put round printed and email reminders, circulate examples of good practice in target setting, hold competitions for the best piece of differentiated planning, speak to individuals and set a date when s/he will be 'coming in to see how it's going for you and what I can do to help'.

Change can sometimes seem elastic, able to be put off to another day when things are less busy (which of course they never are). There is nothing more motivating, therefore, than having a date by which action must be in evidence, and nothing more helpful than occasional reminders of what has already been achieved by others.

'Institutionalising' the change

Institutionalising change means building it into the system in ways that will survive changes of leadership, changes of staff or just the dip in energy that follows the initial enthusiasm involved in doing something new.

As Huberman (1983) said, 'New practices that get built into the training, regulatory, staffing and budgetary cycle survive; others don't.' In relation to SEN systems this means embedding the new way of working into relevant policies (not only SEN, but also curriculum, assessment and professional development policies), into planning formats, into information for parents, into job descriptions, performance management systems and induction for new staff.

A final check

Once you have made a plan for introducing, implementing and embedding changes to your current SEN system, it will be useful to run a final check with the help of the chart in Table 9.2.

The chart identifies five key elements that need to be in place if a complex change is to be successful – vision, skills, incentives and resources.

Where there is no clear vision for what needs to change, and what the new system will look like, the result for all involved (staff, parents, pupils) will be confusion. This points to the need to spend time on self-evaluation, sharing the outcomes and identifying with all stakeholders how they want

VISION	+	SKILLS	+	INCENTIVES	+	RESOURCES	=	CHANGE
	+	SKILLS	+	INCENTIVES	+	RESOURCES	=	CONFUSION
VISION	+		+	INCENTIVES	+	RESOURCES	=	ANXIETY
VISION	+	SKILLS	+		+		=	RESISTANCE
VISION	+	SKILLS	+	INCENTIVES	+		=	FRUSTRATION

TABLE 9.2 Managing complex change

Source: Adapted by Richard Vila, Bayridge Consortium Inc. from Knoster (1991).

things to be in the future. People need 'the big picture' – the background and context for the proposed change, and how things will improve as a result.

Where there is a vision, incentives and resources but those responsible for implementing a change lack the necessary skills, there will be high levels of anxiety. This points to the need for a really good plan for INSET for staff, perhaps in Assessment for Learning, or in understanding and employing data to track and monitor progress, or in inclusive planning. It also means thinking about the skills that pupils will require, along with any necessary development work to ensure that they become confident partners in setting and reviewing targets for their personal and academic development, and communicating to others what their needs are and what forms of support they find helpful.

Where there is vision, and professional development, and resources but no incentives there will be resistance (often subtle, but nevertheless powerful) amongst parents and colleagues in school. The way round this is to highlight very clearly what everyone has to gain from the new system. For parents, this will be better progress for their child – with teachers really having to think about how to teach them rather than handing responsibility over to support staff – and clarity about what extra provision their child can access, over and above the all-important inclusive class and subject teaching. You will need to provide many parents with the evidence, summarised in this book, in *Special educational needs and school improvement* (Gross and White, 2003), and in the National Strategies *Leading on intervention* materials (DfES, 2006d) that the ways of managing things that they have come to expect (attaching TAs to children as if by Velcro, and working on three or four SMART targets) have not, according to national data and Ofsted, led to improved outcomes for pupils with SEN – indeed, rather the reverse. The same arguments can serve to lend staff the incentive to make the change: new systems will mean improved outcomes for children, reflected in the SEF and evident to Ofsted, and linked to rewards inherent in the performance management system. There may be other incentives too, that a creative staff group can come up with as a way of celebrating the effort everyone has put in to make the new system work.

Finally, where there are incentives, coupled with vision and skills, but not enough resources (time or money), the result will be frustration – a familiar scenario for the education staff who have been asked to implement a thousand new initiatives over the last ten years, not all of them adequately funded. As we have seen, proper discussions with senior leaders in school about what time and resources will realistically be required, for the initial preparation period and when the change is implemented, will help reduce staff frustration.

Change and the SENCO/INCO

In all the work you may do with parents, pupils and colleagues to bring about changes in the way SEN is managed in your school, it is important to remember also that a new system may represent considerable change for you too, as SENCO or INCO.

Fundamentally, what you will become is less a manager of paper and meetings, and more of a strategic manager, and a leader of inclusive teaching and learning in your school.

You might want to reflect on what proportion of your time you currently spend on each of these broad activity headings:

- SEN Code of Practice procedures – IEPs, reviews, reports, meetings;
- contributing to year group/subject curriculum planning;
- monitoring – observing lessons and providing feedback;
- managing TAs or other staff;
- supporting school-based staff professional development and work with parents to help them support their child's learning;
- strategic management of SEN – school self-evaluation (including analysing data on the progress of children with SEN), planning and evaluating additional provision, contributing to the school improvement plan;
- teaching children with SEN;
- linking with outside agencies;
- organising resources.

If you record the proportion of time spent on each of these as a chart, it might, perhaps, look like the one in Figure 9.1, with by far the most time spent on processes that research has shown to be least effective in their impact on children's progress. Reducing the number of IEPs in the school should enable you to shift the emphasis, so that your chart might look more like the one in Figure 9.2. Alternatively, if strategic management is really not your thing, and someone else in school carries out that role for inclusion, you could shift the time pattern so that you spend more time teaching

A   SEN Code of Practice procedures –
    IEPs, reviews with parents, reports, meetings
B   Contributing to year group/subject curriculum planning
C   Monitoring – observing lessons and providing feedback
D   Managing TAs or other staff
E   Supporting school-based staff professional development and work
    with parents on how to support their child's learning
F   Strategic management of SEN – School self-evaluation
    (including analysing data on the progress of children with SEN),
    planning and evaluating additional provision, contributing to school
    improvement plan
G   Teaching children with SEN
H   Linking with outside agencies
I   Organising resources

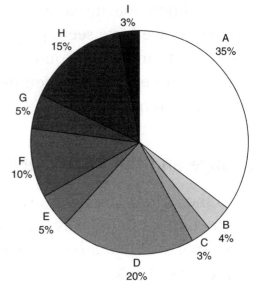

FIGURE 9.1 How do I spend my SENCO/INCO time?

A   SEN Code of Practice procedures –
    IEPs, reviews with parents, reports, meetings
B   Contributing to year group/subject curriculum planning
C   Monitoring – observing lessons and providing feedback
D   Managing TAs or other staff
E   Supporting school-based staff professional development and work
    with parents on how to support their child's learning
F   Strategic management of SEN – School self-evaluation
    (including analysing data on the progress of children with SEN),
    planning and evaluating additional provision, contributing to school
    improvement plan
G   Teaching children with SEN
H   Linking with outside agencies
I   Organising resources

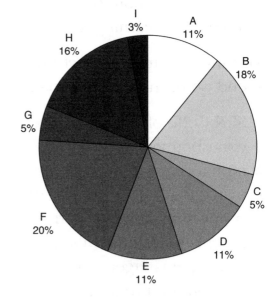

FIGURE 9.2 How do I spend my SENCO/INCO time?

children with SEN directly, using some of the evidence-based intervention programmes described in Chapter 7, or more time supporting family learning and parenting groups or workshops, as described in Chapter 8.

Managing inclusion is a team job, not the role of a single individual. It is up to you and your school to determine how the various roles in relation to SEN and disability are fulfilled, and what your part will be. But shifting away from paper processes to focus on teaching and learning will have big implications for you, whatever the new pattern of your time. It represents a change, and the same conditions that apply to whole-school change also apply to you. You may have a vision for how you want your role to develop in the future, but it is useful to reflect also on what you need in terms of skills, incentives and resources. The incentive of reducing fruitless paperwork may be sufficient, but you may also want to have the effort involved in managing that change recognised and rewarded through your own performance management. You will perhaps be able to articulate to senior leaders the differences you see in your future role, and enter into discussions about how they will be reflected in management structures and pay scales.

Resource implications for your changed role should not be excessive. A reduction in bureaucracy is intended to change the way you use existing time, rather than require lots more. But you will need resources in the form of time at staff meetings or INSET days to introduce staff to new systems, and time identified in their timetables to work with you as you support them in developing their inclusive teaching practice.

Finally, there are likely to be substantial skills implications in a change of role for you. Table 9.3 provides a skills audit to guide you in planning your own professional development. Courses or school-based support on all of this should be available from your local authority, from leading practice schools, or from higher education institutions. In future, it may well be built into mandatory professional qualifications for SENCOs.

Conclusion

Making change happen is difficult. So, however, is the everyday job of SENCOs/INCOs and classroom teachers as they struggle to implement the bureaucratic procedures that currently occupy most of the time and energy available to meet the needs of children with SEN or disabilities. Because of this, change is essential.

Readers of this book will by now understand how fundamental are the changes proposed in the way we manage SEN and disability in schools. The theme may have been how to beat bureaucracy – but it has also been how we might get a better deal for children with SEN or disabilities through the changes we make to our systems. It has been about recognising that, as Charles Desforges (2007) says, 'From the learner's point of view, if educational change does not happen in classrooms then it does not happen.' It has been about shifting effort away from paper and meetings that happen outside the classroom and have little impact on what happens

✓ Tick the column that best fits you

KNOWLEDGE, SKILLS, UNDERSTANDING	I NEED TO LEARN MORE ABOUT THIS	I FEEL PRETTY CONFIDENT IN THIS	I CAN SUPPORT OTHER SENCOS/INCOS IN THIS
Inclusive classroom planning and teaching			
Assessment for learning			
Interpreting and using data on pupil progress			
Provision mapping			
The evidence base for different intervention programmes			
Evaluating the quality and impact of intervention programmes in school			
Providing support to other adults (TAs, learning mentors) delivering intervention programmes			
Undertaking classroom observations and feeding back to staff			
Monitoring planning			
Coaching colleagues			
Providing INSET			
Training pupils in self-advocacy			
Providing workshops and running groups for parents, to help them support their children's language, literacy or mathematics learning			
Providing workshops and running groups for parents, to help them support their children's social and emotional development			

TABLE 9.3 Skills audit for the SENCO/INCO

inside it, onto placing more of the responsibility for meeting individual needs back with the class or subject teacher.

This will only work if we make it easy for these teachers to take on this shift of responsibility. It will only be manageable if the systems we ask them to use for pupils with SEN or disabilities are the *same* as they use for all the class – embedded in their regular target-setting, assessment and curriculum-planning processes.

Taken to the limit, these new systems may eventually mean that, whilst retaining the concept of disability, we can dispense with the more nebulous concept of 'special educational needs' altogether, and simply think about how learning can be personalised for a whole range of children who from time to time require extra responsiveness from us, for all sorts of reasons linked to the experiences they are going through. So far, the notion of special educational needs and the elaborate and separate bureaucracy around it have only served on the whole to marginalise pupils and make them 'someone else's problem'. Integrated, personalised systems will mean they make better progress.

Bureaucracy, it is interesting to reflect, is what others ask of you. *Systems*, however, are what you devise for yourself and your own setting. Schools like the ones in our case studies show us that more effective systems are possible. Such schools would not claim to have beaten bureaucracy, but they do feel that they have held it at bay. Where there is paperwork, it is paperwork that the school sees as meeting the particular needs of their children – not paperwork done for its own sake with little impact on learning. Staff may be working just as hard as ever, but they feel that the actions they take now make sense and will make a difference. As one SENCO put it, 'It's how you *feel* about the time not the actual time that matters.'

The schools described in this book have found new meaning in what they do, as a result of changing the way that key people, particularly the SENCO or INCO, spend their time. Personalisation, provision mapping and new SEN funding systems have created the context that makes this possible. It is up to us all now to follow their lead.

10 | Beating Bureaucracy Toolkit

The materials in this section are available to download from www.routledgeeducation.com/resources/fulton.

Information for Ofsted and Other Outside Agencies

The SEN Code of Practice requires us to have systems in school that fulfil the following purposes:

 Identification – ensuring that children's needs are identified as a result of expressions of concern by teachers or parent/carers

 Assessment – ensuring that assessment takes place, to better understand the barriers to learning and how they might be overcome

 Communication – making sure that all relevant staff and outside agencies know what the child's needs are and what should be done or has been done to support them

 Identifying priorities and setting targets for learning or behaviour; involving pupils

 Planning strategies, in the classroom and elsewhere, to help the child achieve targets

 Reviewing progress and celebrating success

 Engaging parents and carers – agreeing priorities and targets with them, making sure that they know what is being done to help their child and to what effect, suggesting ways in which they can support their child's progress

 Coordinating the actions to be taken by the school and outside agencies

Informing decisions about the allocation of resources – extra adult time and/or physical resources

 Supporting transition – making sure that information about the child's needs is passed on as they move from one class or setting to another.

We agree with Ofsted (2006, *Inclusion: does it matter where pupils are taught?*) that in meeting these functions what makes the difference to better outcomes for pupils with learning difficulties or disabilities is effective target setting within the curriculum or personalised programme, as part of a whole-school policy on assessment.

We have therefore tried wherever possible to support pupils with learning difficulties or disabilities through our regular whole-school systems. It is our policy to write and review separate individual education plans (IEPs) only for children with low-incidence, complex learning difficulties or disabilities, where a number of different agencies are involved. We do not use IEPs for children with high-incidence needs. External research evidence and our own self-evaluation have shown us that these are not effective in raising standards for our pupils or promoting their well-being.

We are also mindful of government guidance:

> Schools do not need to write individual education plans for children with SEN where they have a policy of planning, target setting and recording the progress for all pupils as part of personalised learning that:
>
> ● identifies learning targets for individual pupils;
>
> ● plans additional or different provision from the differentiated curriculum offered to all pupils;
>
> ● reviews provision in the light of individual pupil outcomes.
>
> (IRU, 2007)

The following chart describes the way we manage SEN, and where the evidence is located. Evidence from regular school systems is in italics; evidence from discrete SEN systems is in bold.

Purpose of Code of Practice	Alternative ways of fulfilling these purposes	Beating bureaucracy toolkit
To ensure that children's needs are identified through the expression of concern by parents/carers or teachers.	● Effective tracking of pupil progress. ● Screening procedures (for example, for dyslexia), described in SEN policy.	*SEN register derived from school information management systems* *Regular school tracking systems* **SEN Policy**
To encourage a thorough assessment of the factors which may be contributing to a child's difficulties.	● SENCO trains/coaches colleagues in involving the pupil in identifying strengths, difficulties and what helps. ● Use of information from outside agencies' assessments.	*Regular school conferencing systems*
To ensure that all relevant staff and outside agencies know what the child's needs are.	● Pupil-held Personal Profiles that record strengths, difficulties and what helps. ● Training for pupils in how to communicate their needs.	**Personal Profile or Communication Passport**
To help staff and pupils identify key priorities and learning targets.	● Pupil-owned targets set together by the class or subject teacher and the pupil.	*Regular whole-school systems for setting individual targets*
To ensure that effective strategies are put in place to support the child.	● Strategy sheets for staff. ● SENCO or school-based behaviour/SEAL specialist acts as consultant to colleagues on what works for lower-attaining pupils and those with behavioural, emotional and social difficulties.	*Regular whole-school systems for differentiated curriculum planning* **Strategy sheets** **Provision map**
To review progress and celebrate success.	Assessments used before and after an intervention; effective tracking systems that use NC levels and sublevels; intensification of regular school systems for awards and celebrations.	*Regular whole-school tracking and review systems* **Intervention data collection system**
To ensure that parents/carers know what is being done to help their child, and to what effect. To ensure that parents/carers know what they can do to help their child.	● School SEN policy/school profile contains clear provision map showing the extra provision and what entry levels entitle a child to access that provision. ● Communicating pupils' progress to parents/carers at least twice a year. ● SENCO and curriculum specialists run workshops for parents/families and implement projects (such as paired reading) for specified groups.	**Provision map** Additional agenda items for *progress review meetings with parents and pupils* *Parent workshops listed in school profile and on our website*
To coordinate the actions to be taken by the school and outside agencies.	A column added to provision map, or agency involvement recorded on a single cumulative overview/record of progress.	**Provision map** **Cumulative overview/record of progress**
To ensure that school resources are effectively deployed.	Planning additional provision through a provision map.	**Provision map**
To ensure continuity at times of transition.	Teacher/school passes on class profile pupil Personal Profile and record of additional provision (highlighted, dated provision maps).	**Personal Profile or Communication Passport** **Class Handover Profile** **Provision map**
To demonstrate what has been done at school level before seeking support or funding from outside agencies/local authority.	SENCO/INCO provides copy of extract from school SEN policy on how it fulfils the functions of the Code of Practice without over-reliance on IEPs. They highlight on school's provision map the extra provision the child has received. They send outcomes of regular tracking of progress, examples of differentiated classroom planning, pupil Personal Profile.	**Provision map** **Personal Profile/Communication Passport** *Regular curriculum planning and tracking*

Information for Parents and Carers

Dear Parent

This letter is for parents and carers of children with special educational needs or disabilities. It explains how we will help your child at X school.

We want to make sure that everyone in school understands your child's needs. So we will work with you and your child to write a Communication Passport/Personal Profile that will go to everyone who teaches Y. The Passport/Profile will say what Y is good at, what s/he finds difficult, and what helps him/her to learn.

When teachers plan their lessons they will think about what exactly your child needs to know and learn, what teaching approaches will work best, and what they need to do to overcome any barriers that will stop your child learning. You are very welcome to look at example of teachers' planning. We will also make sure you know about your child's individual targets, which they set with their teachers.

If you would like to help your child reach these targets through home activities we can suggest ideas. Sometimes we organise special events in school – like how to help your child with literacy, or social and emotional learning – that we hope you will come to and find useful.

Y may also have extra 1–1 or small group help with language, literacy, maths, social and emotional or coordination skills. Our school 'provision map' shows what help we provide in each year group. We would like you to see this map. If your child needs this extra help, it will be for a fixed period of time. We will assess progress before and after this extra teaching so that we can tell you what difference it has made.

Class/subject teachers assess each child's overall progress once a term. Progress will be discussed at parents' evenings twice a year. At these meetings we want you to tell us about anything that will help us do a better job to help your child.

But please don't wait for parents' evenings if there is anything you would like to discuss. Just get in touch – your contact person is Z, tel:

With best wishes,

Communication Passport

Child's photograph

NAME:

D.O.B.:

SEN Stage:

SEN Support Began:

Areas of Concern:

WHAT AM I GOOD AT?

WHAT DO I FIND HARD?

WHAT SHOULD TEACHERS AND OTHER PEOPLE IN SCHOOL DO TO HELP ME?

Personal Profile

Name: **Form:**

SEN stage:

Personal Profile

Strengths and interests

Areas of difficulty

Strategies

Inclusive Planning Format

Unit: .... **Date:** .... **Year group:** ....

Key learning objectives: ....

Learning outcome for unit: ....

Planning for inclusion – note here differentiated learning objectives for different individuals and groups, and the teaching approaches and access strategies you will use to overcome barriers to learning.

Differentiated learning objectives

Teaching approaches

Access strategies

SESSION	SHARED LEARNING AND TEACHING	INDEPENDENT LEARNING	PLENARY	ASSESSMENT CRITERIA	GUIDED LEARNING
1					
2					
3					
4					
5					

Medium-term Plan:

YEAR:

TERM:

HIGHLIGHT THE INCLUSIVE TEACHING STRATEGIES RELEVANT TO THE CLASS

Plan seating taking into account needs of pupils with sensory impairment, distractible pupils.	Make tasks more open/closed for different individuals and groups, according to need.
Avoid background noise.	Plan tasks as extended or short for different individuals and groups, according to need.
Check light source in front of me not behind.	Clearly explain and model tasks – check for understanding, task cards or boards as reminders, make time available and expected outcomes clear.
Face pupils when speaking.	Provide resources to help pupils be independent – write down and leave up instructions after saying them, keep relevant material from whole class session on display, provide word lists or mats, dictionaries of terms, glossaries, maths resources such as number lines.
Cue pupils in to what I am going to talk about and cue again when the topic changes.	Vary pupil groupings according to purpose and learning objective.
Clarify, display and refer back to new or difficult vocabulary.	Make arrangements such as buddying, adult support, taping where necessary to ensure that pupils can access written text/instructions.
Break long instructions down into chunks and say one at a time.	Plan alternatives to written recording for those who find this difficult – role play, drama, making posters, video recording, tape recording, dictating to a study buddy, mind mapping, card sorts, matching labels to diagrams or pictures.
Check for understanding of instructions – ask pupil to explain them in their own words.	Use large print worksheets (12–14 point Arial), cream/buff paper.
Jot instructions down on post-it notes or ask a pupil to do this for a study buddy.	Use alternatives to copying notes from the board e.g. photocopy transcript of another pupil's notes.
Use visual supports – pictures, concrete objects, visual timetable.	Provide scaffolding for writing – writing frames, clue cards, choice of words to fill in blanks.
Pitch questions so that they are relevant for learning objectives at different levels.	Plan use of ICT as an access strategy – speech- or sign-supported software, onscreen word banks, predictive word processing, annotating printouts of IWB pages.
Give time/support before responses are required – personal thinking time, partner talk, persisting with progressively more scaffolding until child can answer correctly.	Give pupils opportunity to feed back in plenary in variety of media.
Use buddying for seating and paired/partner work – more settled pupil paired with a child who finds concentration difficult, more able with less able.	Give pupils time to copy down homework or provide it on a sheet.
Plan pre-tutoring by TA for individuals/groups, where this will help them to access the lesson.	
Make sure TA knows learning objective for any pupil(s) they will be supporting.	
Use encapsulation – tell class the three main points lesson will cover, teach them, recap on them at end of lesson.	

UNIT (Weeks)	LEARNING OBJECTIVES (for pupils above/at/below and where appropriate well above/ well below age-related expectations)	CHILDREN'S TARGETS (for pupils above/at/below and where appropriate well above/well below age-related expectations)	SUCCESS CRITERIA	FOCUS OF USE AND APPLICATION
1				
2				
3				
4				
5				

Attention Deficit Hyperactivity Disorder (ADHD)

Please use the highlighted strategies with ... (Pupil) in ... (Form)

Seat pupil near the front with their back to the class, between two good role models and well away from areas other pupils need to walk through.
Establish a quiet place where pupil can go to work.
Allow pupil to fiddle with a piece of blu-tac, rubber band, squeeze ball or another chosen object.
Make tasks short, with frequent breaks and opportunities to move around.
Give instructions simply and clearly. Make sure the pupil is looking at you first. Check that he or she has understood them.
Use a kitchen or sand timer to help pupil complete a task in a specified period of time.
Aim for a ratio of four positive comments to one negative and teach pupil how to reward themselves: 'You managed to concentrate on your work very well just then; give yourself a pat on the back.'
Devise a private signal system to let the pupil know when they are off task or behaving inappropriately.
Use a planned reward system.
Teach a relaxation strategy like slow breathing and cue pupil when they need to use it.
Teach/use clear classroom routines, e.g. have all pupils hold an object when it is their turn to talk. Display classroom rules and routines for pupil to refer to. Illustrate them visually – for example, use a traffic-light system to indicate whether pupils can talk or not, or symbols for different noise levels (partner voices, group voices, classroom voice, playground voices).
When pupil is misbehaving: ● Say what you want him or her to do, rather than what you don't – 'N., I want you to keep your hands in your lap' instead of 'N, stop bothering P'. ● Label the behaviour but not the pupil – not 'You big bully' but 'N, bullying is not allowed in our school'. ● Remind pupil of a rule, rather than telling them off – 'N, our rule is we put up our hand to answer', or make a point of praising a pupil who is keeping the rule – 'A, I like the way you put your hand up when you knew the answer'. ● Use the language of choice, reminding pupils of the consequences of the various behavioural choices open to them.
To help pupil work independently: ● Actively teach core routines for certain tasks, having pupil practise them with progressively less help until they can quickly tell you and show you what they have to do if you ask them to do that type of task. ● Give independent tasks that have previously been modelled for the whole class. ● Give clear guidelines: 'I expect you to have produced at least three lines by ten past ten; I will be asking you then to share these with your writing partner.' ● Use visual prompts in the form of pictorial task cards. ● Provide support in the form of writing frames, word mats, relevant classroom displays, and prompts such as a card with ideas for 'Five things to do if you are stuck with your work'.
Ask another pupil or a small group to buddy the pupil who is having difficulties, praising them when they achieve easily reachable behavioural targets.

Autistic Spectrum Disorder

Please use the highlighted strategies with ... (Pupil) in ... (Form)

Prepare the pupil before the session/lesson by outlining what it will be about.
Support oral presentations/explanations with charts, diagrams, pictures, real objects or mime.
Set tasks with clear goals and write worksheets in step-by-step form.
If pupil becomes anxious allow him/her to remove self to an agreed calm-down area.
Seat pupil in an area of classroom free from busy displays and distractions.
Teach/use clear classroom routines, e.g. have all pupils hold an object when it is their turn to talk. Display classroom rules and routines, illustrated by pictures, for pupil to refer to. Illustrate them visually – for example, use a traffic-light system to indicate whether pupils can talk or not, or symbols for different noise levels (partner voices, group voices, classroom voice, playground voices).
Use a visual way of showing the pupil what they/the class will be doing, such as a sequenced series of pictures (a visual timetable), clockface divided into sections, or written list.
Use timeline of events → → that branches ↕ to show where pupil will have to make choices.
Use short simple instructions. Give one at a time and check for understanding. Repeat instructions in same words rather than different ones. Write instructions down as a list for pupil to tick off when completed.
Use pupil's name before asking a question or giving an instruction.
Avoid or explain metaphorical language and idiom like 'pull your socks up', 'it's raining cats and dogs', 'in a minute'.
Explain any changes of routine to the pupil in advance.
Involve the pupil by asking direct, concrete questions at their level of understanding.
Support writing with writing frames, templates (e.g. writing up a science experiment), mind maps, gapped handouts.
Allow pupil to work alone rather than in a group where possible. If in a group, give clear roles within the group and put the rules and roles into writing.
Use visual prompts on cards or photos, or consistent non-verbal signs (sit, look, listen, hand up, wait, quiet) to show pupil the social behaviours expected.
Prevent repetitive questioning by giving pupil a set number of question cards to give you each time they ask a question – when cards are gone, no more questions.
Don't ask the pupil to talk or write about imagined experiences.
Avoid tasks which depend on empathy (e.g. in literature, history, geography, PSHE and citizenship).
Set explicit and clear expectations e.g. how many lines to write, how many questions to answer, how long to listen (use timer).
Put a green 'start' dot on the pupil's book and a line to show where to finish. Use in and out boxes for work to be done and work that is finished.
Provide pupil with a symbol card to display when he or she wants help.
Expect to teach pupil social skills e.g. what to say/do when praised, how to ask for help. Always tell the pupil what to do rather than what not to do.
Provide a structure for unstructured time e.g. chess club rather than breaktime outside.
Model to the pupil that making mistakes is OK and a part of the learning process.
Use incentives based on pupil's interests e.g. a pause every hour to focus on their interest or obsession, once they have completed their work.
If pupil goes off at a tangent, direct conversation back to the topic in hand; 'Right now we are talking about volcanoes'.
Use immediate and individualised reward systems e.g. collecting a number of stickers.

Behavioural, Emotional and Social Difficulties (BESD)

Please use the highlighted strategies with ... (Pupil) in ... (Form)

Seat pupil by a more settled peer.
If pupil becomes wound up/anxious, allow him/her to remove self to an agreed calm-down area.
Make tasks short, with frequent breaks and opportunities to move around.
Remember that children (and adults) who are stressed find it hard to take in and remember complex information; make instructions short and clear. When pupil is experiencing emotional turbulence or anxiety, provide low-key tasks and increased structure and predictability in the classroom environment.
Set tasks with clear goals, outputs and timescales.
Teach/use clear classroom routines e.g. have all pupils hold an object when it is their turn to talk. Display classroom rules and routines for pupil to refer to. Illustrate them visually – for example, use a traffic-light system to indicate whether pupils can talk or not, or symbols for different noise levels (partner voices, group voices, classroom voice, playground voices).
Expect to teach pupil specific behavioural skills e.g. how to ask for help.
When pupil is misbehaving: ● Say what you want him or her to do, rather than what you don't – 'N, I want you to keep your hands in your lap' instead of 'N, stop bothering P'.   ● Label the behaviour but not the pupil – not 'You big bully' but 'N, bullying is not allowed in our school'.   ● Remind pupils of a rule, rather than telling them off – 'N, our rule is we put up our hand to answer', or make a point of praising a pupil who is keeping the rule – 'A, I like the way you put your hand up when you knew the answer'.   ● Use the language of choice, reminding pupils of the consequences of the various behavioural choices open to them.
Make an effort to 'catch the pupil being good' and praise them. Aim for a ratio of four positive comments to one negative and teach pupil how to reward themselves: 'You managed to concentrate on your work very well just then; give yourself a pat on the back'.
Devise a private signal system to let the pupil know when they are off task or behaving inappropriately.
Use a planned reward system for appropriate behaviour.
Enhance access to ICT – use of the internet to research a topic, access to predictive word processing software and onscreen word grids to support writing, opportunities to create presentations.
To help pupil work independently: ● Actively teach core routines for certain tasks, having pupil practise them with progressively less help until they can quickly tell you and show you what they have to do if you ask them to do that type of task.   ● Set independent tasks that have previously been modelled for the whole class.   ● Give clear guidelines: 'I expect you to have produced at least three lines by ten past ten; I will be asking you then to share these with your writing partner.'   ● Use visual prompts in the form of pictorial task cards.   ● Provide support in the form of writing frames, word mats, relevant classroom displays, and prompts such as a card with ideas for 'Five things to do if you are stuck with your work'.

Take steps to build pupil's self-confidence:

- Find out what they know about or are good at, and have them share this with the rest of the class or school.
- Give them responsibilities, for example organising a lunchtime or after-school club, being a playground buddy, helping those who are new to the school.
- Have them keep records of new things they learn and can do.
- Ask them to tutor another pupil with their work.
- Photocopy good pieces of work for them to take home.

Take special steps to build the relationship with the pupil:

- Take extra care to greet the pupil each day and say a word or two individually to them.
- Have lunch with the pupil from time to time. Try to involve them in a lunchtime or after-school club that you run.
- Invite them to help you with daily tasks.
- Listen without giving advice or opinions; show that you understand how the pupil feels... '*That must have made you very angry/upset.*'
- When things go wrong, reject the behaviour, not the pupil ... '*This is not the behaviour I expect to see from someone as kind and helpful as you.*'
- Don't be afraid to tell the pupil you like them and that what happens to them matters to you... '*You really matter to me and it's important to me that you do well this year.*'

Organise time – perhaps during registration – for a teaching assistant to chat with the pupil, giving them a chance to talk about anything that may be troubling them and get themselves ready for learning.

Ask another pupil or a small group to buddy the pupil who is having difficulties, praising them when they achieve easily reachable behavioural targets.

Deploy a teaching assistant to model, coach and reinforce group work skills when the pupil is working collaboratively with other pupils.

Dyslexia

Please use the highlighted strategies with ... (Pupil) in ... (Form)

Have pupils work in pairs – dyslexic pupil who has good ideas but difficulty with spelling and handwriting with a pupil who is good at writing but not so strong on ideas.
Have any text that the pupil will struggle with read to them by a 'study buddy' or TA.
Avoid asking pupil to copy from board – have them work with a study buddy, or quickly jot things down for them, or use a photocopied transcript.
Be aware that the pupil may find it hard to hold questions, information or instructions in their head for long enough to act on them, and: ● repeat instructions/questions; ● 'chunk' them rather than saying in one long string; ● jot them down on a sticky note, or encourage the pupil to do so; ● allow time for processing (for example paired discussion with a partner before putting hands up).
Be aware that dyslexic pupils may know something one day and forget it the next, may lose or forget equipment they need, or may forget what they are supposed to be doing in the course of a lesson. Avoid criticism when this happens; instead, talk with them about strategies they can use to help them remember things.
Use ICT supports – audiotaped texts, laptop, predictive word processing, speech-supported texts, spellcheckers, mind-mapping software.
Mark for content rather than presentation. When marking, praise for two correct spellings, target two incorrect spellings and use these errors as teaching points. Suggest a way of avoiding the mistake in future – for example, the similarity of the spelling to other known words, or 'the tricky bit' that has to be learned.
Enable pupil to record their ideas using alternatives to writing: PowerPoint presentations, making posters, oral presentations, dramatic reconstructions, mind maps, matching labels to pictures/diagrams/maps, sorting statements or pictures into categories.
Scaffold writing: ● Provide writing frames and templates (e.g. writing up a science experiment) to help structure thinking. ● Supply prompt sheets: questions to answer, key words to build each section or paragraph around, sentences or paragraphs to put in correct order, paragraph openings. ● Provide clue cards. ● Use cloze procedure (where the pupil fills in missing words in text). ● Print off an IWB page used in whole-class session and have pupils add to it/annotate.
Do not expect pupil to remember easily sequences such as days of the week, months of the year, the alphabet, times tables, number facts. Provide aids (for example, a pocket alphabet or calendar, table squares, calculator).
Avoid embarrassing pupil by asking them to read aloud in front of others, unless they volunteer.
Overcome problems in learning by rote by helping pupil recognise patterns, use mnemonics, or use memory strategies that create relationships between items in a list in order to aid recall.
Allow extra time to complete tasks and be aware of the fatigue the pupil may experience because of the amount of effort they have to put into learning.
Teach pupil strategies to improve organisation, such as diaries, workplans, checklists of equipment that they have to bring to school each day.
Provide the pupil with a study pack – spellchecker, highlighter pens, glue sticks, post-it notes, a line tracker for following text, blank audio tapes, index cards for subject vocabulary or spelling mnemonics, dictionary sheet of high-frequency words, alphabet strip, memory jogger card for b/d confusion, sticky labels to use to correct or conceal, a tables square, a calendar, a calculator.
Write down homework for pupil, or give it on a pre-printed sticky label or sheet that they can stick into their book, or record your instructions on a dictaphone. Allocate a homework buddy they can ring if they have forgotten what to do ('phone a friend').

Hearing Impairment

Please use the highlighted strategies with ... (Pupil) in ... (Form)

Use TA for pre-tutoring – preparing pupil for lesson e.g. explaining new words and concepts.
Seat pupil at front where able to read text, hear and lip-read.
Position sign supporters alongside teacher where pupil can see both.
Ensure light is on teacher's face, i.e. light source behind pupil – don't stand with your back to a window.
Face pupil when speaking to facilitate lip-reading; repeat any instructions that have been given when the pupil could not see the speaker; avoid writing on board or IWB while speaking as you will not be facing pupil.
Don't make the pupil concentrate on lip-reading for too long without a break.
When other pupils contribute, ensure that they speak one at a time. Paraphrase their contributions back to the class.
Speak clearly, naturally and at a normal rate – shouting or exaggerated 'mouthing' distorts normal lip patterns.
Minimise background noise e.g. noisy heater, buzzing light. Make other pupils aware of need for a quiet working environment.
Use short simple instructions. Give one at a time and check for understanding. Repeat instructions first in same words, but then if these are not understood substitute different words.
Support oral presentations/explanations with charts, diagrams, pictures, real objects or mime. Write topics or headings on the board as you introduce them.
Prepare the pupil before the session/lesson by outlining what it will be about.
Use pupil's name before asking a question or giving an instruction.
Cue pupil in to a change of topic of conversation presentation – say 'now we are going to talk about...'.
Question pupil after some other pupils have given examples of what is required.
Accept pupil's spoken utterances but rephrase and give them back in a grammatically correct version.
Be aware that independent writing will reflect the pupil's spoken language levels and will not necessarily be grammatically correct.
Support writing with writing frames and lists of vocabulary to choose from.
Put up a list of key vocabulary for a particular topic or lesson and teach the meaning of each word.
Use a range of ways of recording so that learning is not limited by the pupil's ability to write full English sentences: ● bullet points and mind maps; ● ordering tasks – for example, ordering cut-out words to make a sentence, or sentences to make a sequence of instructions; ● matching tasks, such as matching labels to pictures/diagrams/maps; ● cloze procedure, where they fill in missing words in text; ● annotating a printout of IWB page; ● PowerPoint presentations; ● making posters, oral presentations, dramatic reconstructions.
Agree private signal that pupil can use to show you when they have not understood.
Try to use video with subtitles; if not available, allow pupil to borrow video material after lesson to go through it again. Don't ask pupil to make notes while watching a video.
Allow extra time to complete tasks and be aware of the fatigue the pupil may experience because of the amount of effort they have to put in to listening.

Learning Difficulties

Please use the highlighted strategies with ... (Pupil) in ... (Form)

Use TA for pre-tutoring – preparing pupil for a task so that they come to it already knowing the key vocabulary and concepts.
Link new learning to what pupil already knows – e.g. start lesson with class mind map of what they already know about a subject.
Tell pupils the three key points of the lesson, teach them and recap on them at the end.
Break new learning down into small steps.
Provide multiple examples of new concepts, and take these examples from children's own real-life experience rather than talking in the abstract.
Use visual and kinaesthetic learning – learning from pictures, diagrams, mind maps, using practical equipment, handling objects, moving and doing rather than sitting.
Use scaffolding – having a peer or adult work alongside the pupil at first, then gradually withdraw as confidence grows, or having pupil finish a task that has already been part-done for them.
Use short simple instructions. Give one at a time and check for understanding. Write down and leave up instructions after saying them.
Question pupil after some other pupils have given examples of what is required.
Give pupil time to think, or to talk to a partner before answering a question, or say 'I'm going to come back to you in a minute to ask you xxxx.'.
If pupil can't answer a question, scaffold/support till they can rather than saying 'Can anyone help x?'; echo back the pupil's answers in expanded form.
Buddy the pupil with a more able peer.
Have any text that the pupil will struggle with read to them by a 'study buddy' or TA.
Put up a list of key vocabulary for a particular topic or lesson and teach the meaning of each word.
To help pupil extract the salient points from information that they are given, use highlighter pens or provide cards telling them what they have to look out for on a visit, in a text or from sources such as film.
Make learning strategies explicit by 'thinking aloud' yourself.
Help pupil develop and generalise effective learning strategies – when successful, ask them to identify what they did to solve the problem/find the information.
Model to the pupil that making mistakes is OK and a part of the learning process.
Agree a private signal that the pupil can use to show you when they have not understood.
Pair a higher-attaining group with a lower-attaining one and provide a range of collaborative activities so that pupils can help one another.
Prepare pupils for writing – have them work in a group with you or a TA to rehearse orally what they want to say, then plan the writing together.
Enable pupil to record their ideas using alternatives to writing: PowerPoint presentations, making posters, oral presentations, dramatic reconstructions, mind maps, matching labels to pictures/diagrams/maps, sorting statements or pictures into categories.
Use software that supports writing, with onscreen word grids from which they can choose the words they need.
Scaffold writing: ● Provide writing frames and templates (e.g. writing up a science experiment) to help structure thinking. ● Supply prompt sheets: questions to answer, key words to build each section or paragraph around, sentences or paragraphs to put in correct order, paragraph openings. ● Provide clue cards. ● Use cloze procedure (where the pupil fills in missing words in text). ● Print off an IWB page used in whole-class session and have pupils add to it/annotate.
Give homework instructions on a sheet and make time to explain them. Allocate a homework buddy to ring if they need help ('phone a friend').

Motor Coordination and Associated Difficulties*

Please use the highlighted strategies with ... (Pupil) in ... (Form)

Minimise need for extensive handwritten recording – use ICT (predictive word processor, onscreen word banks, graphics packages), bullet points, mind mapping, flow charts, gapped handouts, buddy acting as scribe, photocopied transcripts of notes, pre-prepared post-its with information the pupil can pick up and place on the page, printout of IWB page for pupil to annotate.
Design worksheets so that the layout is uncluttered. Use buff or cream paper, large print (12–14 point) and a clear font such as Arial. Set information out in panels. Signpost sections with key words, symbols and pictures. Put important information in bold or colour.
Check seating – desktop should be at elbow height, pupil should be able to sit right back in their chair with knees bending back at right angles and **feet flat on the floor**. Put box or large book under feet if necessary.
Use aids supplied – portable writing slope, clipboards to attach paper to, non-slip mats, repositional glue sticks used to anchor paper or other materials, ruler and paper backed with Dycem, small tray for equipment, triangular and thick-barrelled pencils/pens/paintbrushes or smooth-flowing rollerball pens, two handled/loop handled/spring-loaded scissors, transparent pencil case, templates and stencils (e.g. map outlines) for drawing.
Use a reminder handwriting alphabet and numeral formation guide at top of desk.
Use larger-lined book or paper, columns or boxes to place numbers in, squared paper.
Provide the pupil with study packs – everything they need for each subject/lesson in a separate folder, plus pack of highlighter pens, post-it notes, a line tracker for following text, various sized card 'windows' to limit vision to one area of page, sticky labels to use to correct or conceal.
Teach pupil strategies to improve organisation, such as diaries, workplans, checklists of equipment that they have to bring to school each day.
Help pupil follow text on board or IWB by writing/highlighting alternate lines in different colours.
Enlarge pages from textbooks, cut out the particular exercise needed and then mount it on a separate page.
If the pupil needs to work through a series of questions, help them keep their place by using a paper clip or blob of blu-tac to indicate which question they are on.
Pair pupil with a more coordinated study buddy for work involving fine motor skills.
Provide pre-prepared formats (diagrams, charts and graphs) on which pupil can record information.
Teach pupil to talk themselves through visual and spatial tasks – e.g. learn verbal model for letter formation ('b – start at top, down, up, round'), translate maths calculations into verbal problems.
Seat pupil away from distractions with plenty of space each side of them – pupil should have writing arm on the outside edge of shared table. Pupil should be able to see the teacher without turning their body.
Avoid criticism if pupil looks untidy.
Choose resources that don't require manipulation (e.g. number line rather than counters in maths).
Colour code spatially confusable items e.g. x sign in one colour, + sign in another.
Allow ample rest periods as concentration and motor effort is demanding and pupil is easily fatigued.
Write down homework for pupil or give it on a sheet or pre-printed sticky label that they can put in their book. Accept homework written down by parents.

* See also speech and language – expression – if speech articulation is a problem.

Speech and Language Difficulty

Please use the highlighted strategies with ... (Pupil) in ... (Form)

Use TA for pre-tutoring – preparing pupil for a task so that they come to it already knowing the key vocabulary and concepts.
Begin work on a new topic with pupil's existing knowledge and experiences – make a mind map or other visual representation of what they already know.
When you start a new topic, develop a class chart of the vocabulary that pupils will find useful or need to learn.
Use cued listening – give pupil a small number of questions that they will have to answer after listening to teacher presentation or video input.
Use pupil's name before asking a question or giving an instruction.
Give directions before, but not during an activity.
Keep verbal instructions simple, and in the order you want them carried out. Be aware of how many 'information-carrying' words you are using: 'Get your **maths book** from the pile on **my desk**; on a **clean page, write** the **date** and then **copy down** the **calculations on the board'** has more information-carrying words than many adults will be able to remember.
Give pupil time (at least 10 seconds) to respond and then, if necessary, repeat what you said. Use the same words unless you think the vocabulary was too difficult to understand.
Check for understanding – ask the pupil to tell you what they have to do.
Agree a private signal that pupil can use to show you when they have not understood.
Support your oral presentations/explanations with pictures, real objects or mime.
Use symbols to support spoken language and text (www.widgit.com).
Use visual summaries of discussions – mind maps, flow charts, diagrams, comic-strip format.
Put up a list of key vocabulary for a particular topic or lesson and teach the meaning of each word.
Cue pupil into a change of topic of conversation/presentation – say 'Now we are going to talk about...'
Question pupil after some other pupils have given examples of what is required.
Give pupil time to think, or to talk to a partner before answering a question, or say 'I'm going to come back to you in a minute to ask you xxxx. But first I'm going to ask y a question.'
If pupil can't answer a question, scaffold/support till they can rather than saying 'Can anyone help x?'.
Use a hierarchy of questions – start with an open question ('What do you think might happen next?'), then if support is needed frame the question as alternatives ('Do you think x or y?').
If you cannot understand what the pupil has said, do not pretend that you have – ask for repetition in different words.
Encourage conversation by commenting rather than asking too many questions.
Pair pupil with a study buddy to repeat instructions and demonstrate tasks.
Accept pupil's spoken utterances but rephrase and give them back in a grammatically correct and expanded version.
Support oral work with talk frames/key phrases ('First ... next ... finally', 'I think ... but on the other hand').
Support writing with writing frames and lists of vocabulary to choose from.
Use a range of ways of recording so that learning is not limited by the pupil's ability to write full English sentences: ● bullet points and mind maps; ● ordering tasks – for example, ordering cut-out words to make a sentence, or sentences to make a sequence of instructions; ● matching tasks, such as matching labels to pictures/diagrams/maps; ● cloze procedure, where they fill in missing words in text; ● annotating a printout of IWB page; ● PowerPoint presentations; ● making posters, oral presentations, dramatic reconstructions.
Provide the pupil with a study pack – glossaries of key subject vocabulary, highlighter pens, glue stick, post-it notes, index cards to make their own mind maps/cartoon strips/key word lists, templates for writing up science experiments etc.
Allow extra time to complete tasks and be aware of the fatigue that the pupil may experience because of the amount of effort that they have to put into learning.
Write down homework for pupil, or give it on a pre-printed sticky label or sheet that they can stick into their book, or record your instructions on a dictaphone. Allocate a homework buddy to ring if they have forgotten what to do ('phone a friend').

Visual Impairment

Please use the highlighted strategies with ... (Pupil) in ... (Form)

Use TA for pre-tutoring – preparing pupil for lesson e.g. explaining concepts that rely on vision for understanding.
Don't ask pupil if they can see what is on board/IWB etc. (they may not know) – check by using symbols that pupil knows then use same-size font/background/colour as the symbols you have checked.
Avoid pupil having to look directly into a light source – do not sit or stand with the light behind you.
Use clear, well-spaced print that is suitably contrasted with the background according to individual pupil's needs (for x, y colour on z background). Use non-glossy, non-reflective paper. Use photocopies of masters not of faint blurred versions.
Give verbal information to replace/supplement information from pictures, questions, facial expression.
Use tactile experience to replace/supplement visual input (for example, if class is watching sugar cubes dissolve in a beaker, pupil can put their hand in beaker and feel it dissolve).
Ensure pupil has an individual copy of print material being read in the appropriate format (e.g. large print, Braille). This applies to information on classroom walls too (posters, key vocabulary lists).
Say pupil's name before asking a question or giving an instruction and indicate who is talking in a class discussion.
Provide pupil with own copy of materials to be written on board or IWB; read aloud what you or other pupils are writing up.
Use larger-lined paper, columns or boxes to place numbers in, squared paper. Have pupil use dark pen instead of pencil.
When alerting pupils to an action, artefact, illustration or example don't just point – describe what you want the pupils to take notice of and if necessary describe what it is.
Ensure pupil uses aids supplied – such as CCTV, hand held and portable video magnifiers, book stands, speech output software, digital accessible information system.
Ensure pupil has access to the most appropriate medium for recording work (heavily lined paper, laptop, Braille machine, tape recorder, headphones, digital accessible information system). Access to power supply or space for Braille machine may be required.
Ensure pupil has all the curriculum materials and equipment required to hand and that the materials are organised and contained consistently and securely (use Dycem non-slip mat, a high-sided tray or container with compartments).
Raise position of text (e.g. use sloping desk, reading stands).
Minimise need for extensive handwritten recording – use ICT (predictive word processor, onscreen word banks, graphics packages), bullet points, mind mapping, flow charts, gapped handouts, buddy acting as scribe, photocopied transcripts of notes, printout of IWB page for pupil to annotate.
Use tactile indicators – blu-tac, paper clips – to help pupil find information, locate where they need to be on page, keep track of which question they are on in a series.
Allow extra time to complete tasks and be aware of the fatigue the pupil may experience because of the amount of effort they have to put into learning.
Record your homework instructions on a dictaphone. Allocate a homework buddy they can ring if they have forgotten what to do ('phone a friend').

Provision Map (Primary)

PROVISION	YR	Y1	Y2	Y3	Y4	Y5	Y6
Language intervention							
Literacy intervention							
Maths intervention							
Coordination programme							
EAL provision							
1–1 SEAL work							
Small group SEAL work							
In-class support							
Attendance provision							
Gifted and talented provision							
Other							

Provision Map (Secondary)

PROVISION	Y7	Y8	Y9	Y10	Y11
Targeted literacy intervention					
Targeted maths intervention					
Targeted science intervention					
Further SEN literacy intervention					
Further SEN mathematics intervention					
EAL provision					
1–1 mentoring for aspirations/engagement with learning					
SEAL focus groups					
1–1 SEAL work (counselling, solution focused etc.)					
In-class support for individuals					
Extended school provision					
Gifted and talented provision					
Other					

Cumulative Tracking and Intervention Record

Expected English and maths level for age group shaded

* Child's reading level ● Writing level + Maths level ° Speaking and listening level

NC LEVEL	Y1			Y2			Y3			Y4			Y5			Y6		
	Term 1	Term 2	Term 3	Term 1	Term 2	Term 3	Term 1	Term 2	Term 3	Term 1	Term 2	Term 3	Term 1	Term 2	Term 3	Term 1	Term 2	Term 3
5A																		
5B																		
5C																		
4A																		
4B																		
4C																		
3A																		
3B																		
3C																		
2A																		
2B																		
2C																		
1A																		
1B																		
1C																		
P8																		
P7																		
P6																		
P5																		
P4																		
P1–3																		

Interventions in place

Progress Review Meetings with Parents and Pupils (SEN or Disability)

> **Pre-meeting information for class teacher or form tutor to gather**
>
> ✓ Notes of last meeting
> ✓ Progress against termly National Curriculum sub-level targets/P levels in the core subjects
> ✓ Achievement of curricular and personal targets
> ✓ Progress in relevant behavioural, organisational, study and 'learning-to-learn' skills
> ✓ 'Before' and 'after' assessments showing impact of any interventions used (literacy, language, mathematics, social and emotional, motor coordination, other)
> ✓ Evidence of differentiation of class/subject teacher planning

Agenda

- Have we all completed the actions we agreed at our last meeting?
- How good is x's progress against termly National Curriculum sub-level targets/P levels in the core subjects?
- Is x achieving his/her curricular and personal targets? How good is progress in relevant behavioural, organisational, study and 'learning-to-learn' skills?
- What has been the impact of any interventions we have used? Are any further interventions needed?
- How have we adapted our classroom planning to meet x's needs?
- What is helping x to make progress?
- What is getting in the way?
- What can we do about it?

Notes

Actions agreed

Date: Signed:

Intervention Plan

Name of provision	**NURTURE GROUP**
Aims of the programme	To develop the skills young children need in order to learn: the ability to settle, listen, concentrate, share and make friends.
Description of programme	Small class of up to 12 children taught by a teacher and a TA. Children register with their mainstream class and spend some time there each week, but spend most of the day in the nurture group room. This is designed to replicate a nurturing home, with areas themed around home, kitchen, work and play.
Target group	Children who are unable to respond in a mainstream class, are seriously disruptive or withdrawn, and failing to learn because their basic emotional and social needs have not been met in their early years. Usually Reception age.
Entry level	Scores on Boxall Profile that indicate developmental levels well below those expected of competently functioning children, or behaviours which are preventing the child making progress both academically and socially.
Exit level	Teacher judgement based on changes to Boxall Profile or use of Nurture Group Reintegration Readiness Scale (Doyle, 2001) – numerical score 218 (70%) or above.
Length of intervention	Two to five terms.
Frequency	Daily.
Delivered by	Teacher and TA or nursery nurse.
Suggested start date	Any time.
Groupings	Group of up to 12.
Assessment method	Boxall Profile.
Monitoring arrangements	HT/Deputy HT observation using checklist of criteria for effective nurture groups from Nurture Group Network.

Task	Date/Information	Checklist tick when completed
Identify children to be assessed on Boxall Profile	Names:	
Set a date for assessment	Date:	
Select children for the group	Names:	
Set a date for a parent meeting	Date:	
Set a date for the intervention programme to begin	Date:	
Set a date for HT/Deputy HT observation		
Set a date for post-programme assessments	Date:	
Set dates for 3- and 6-month follow-up assessments	Date:	
Complete evaluation and disseminate outcomes to SLT	Date:	

Intervention Plan

Name of provision	**TALKING PARTNERS**
Aims of the programme	To improve speaking and listening skills across the curriculum.
Description of programme	The programme provides structured activities which encourage and support pupils' developing oral language skills in a variety of situations. Activities particularly support achievement of NLS objectives.
Target group	End of FS to Year 3.
Entry level	Teacher assessment based upon child's oracy across the curriculum.
Exit level	
Length of intervention	10 weeks.
Frequency	3 × 20 mins weekly.
Delivered by	TA, who has been trained to deliver the programme.
Suggested start date	Flexible.
Groupings	Maximum 3.
Assessment method	Renfrew Language Scales pre- and post-intervention (grammar and information).
	Observation sheet.
	Measure against speaking and listening curricular target.
	Child summary sheets.
Monitoring arrangements	INCO to observe TA twice during the 10-week programme

Task	Date/Information	Checklist tick when completed
Identify children to be screened	Names:	
Set a date for screening	Date:	
Select children for the group	Names:	
Fix a timetable for the sessions each week	Times:	
Allocate half a day of preparation time for the TA	Date:	
Decide where the sessions will take place	Location:	
Fix a time for the weekly teacher/ TA review session	Time:	
Set a date for the intervention programme to begin	Date:	
Set a date for the parent meeting	Date:	
Set a date for the progress checks during the programme	Date:	
Set dates for INCO to observe session	Date:	
Set a date for post-programme assessments	Date:	
Complete evaluation and disseminate outcomes to SLT	Date:	

Intervention Plan

Name of provision	**READING RECOVERY**
Aims of the programme	To generate accelerated learning back to the appropriate NLS Framework for teaching objectives.
Description of programme	Reading Recovery is a Wave 3 intervention programme for children who have made very little progress in reading and writing during their first year in school. It involves a daily 1-to-1 lesson with a highly trained teacher.
Target group	Year 1/Year 2.
Entry level	Lowest-attaining pupils.
Exit level	Age appropriate National Curriculum levels in reading and writing.
Length of intervention	12 to 20 weeks.
Frequency	30 mins daily.
Delivered by	Teacher with Reading Recovery teaching qualification.
Suggested start date	After the child has been in school for 3 terms.
Groupings	1.
Assessment method	Book band level/running record.
	Writing sample.
	BAS reading test.
	Reading Recovery Observation Survey.
Monitoring arrangements	Reading Recovery teacher to be observed teaching by LA Teacher Leader.

Task	Date/Information	Checklist tick when completed
Identify children to be screened	Names:	
Set a date for screening	Date:	
Select children to take part	Names:	
Fix a timetable for the sessions each week	Times:	
Decide where the sessions will take place	Location:	
Fix date for LA Teacher Leader to monitor teaching	Date:	
Set a date for the intervention programme to begin	Date:	
Set times for liaison with class teacher		
Set dates for post-programme assessments	Date:	
Set dates for 3- and 6-month follow-up assessments	Date:	
Complete evaluation and disseminate outcomes to SLT	Date:	

Intervention Plan

Name of provision	**YEAR 3 LITERACY SUPPORT**
Aims of the programme	To ensure that in Year 3 term 3, all children are working at the appropriate objectives and are able to participate fully in the daily literacy hour with their peers. The aim of the intervention is to accelerate the progress of children who need additional support in reading and writing. These sessions are additional to the daily literacy hour.
Description of programme	Revisit NLS objectives for Year 2 and 3 terms 1 and 2. The programme covers spelling, reading and writing and has a strong focus on developing independence.
Target group	Year 3.
Entry level	2c (Purple book band).
Exit level	Module 1 = 2c. Module 2 = 2b. Module 3 = 2a.
Length of intervention	Module 1 = 6 weeks. Module 2 = 4 weeks. Module 3 = 6 weeks.
Frequency	30 mins per session.
Delivered by	TA, who has been trained to deliver the programme, delivers 3 sessions per week. Teacher delivers guided reading and guided writing.
Suggested start date	Spring term.
Groupings	Maximum 6.
Monitoring arrangements	Literacy coordinator to observe 2 sessions.
Assessment method	4 screenings.
	Book band level/running record.
	Writing sample.
	Flow chart – entry and exit.
	Progress checks.

Task	Date/Information	Checklist tick when completed
Identify children to be screened	Names:	
Set a date for screening	Date:	
Select children for the group	Names:	
Fix a timetable for the sessions each week	Times:	
Allocate half a day of preparation time for the TA	Date:	
Decide where the sessions will take place	Location:	
Fix a time for the weekly teacher/ TA review session	Time:	
Set a date for the parent meeting	Date:	
Set a date for the intervention programme to begin	Date:	
Set a date for the progress checks during the programme	Date:	
Set dates for LITCO to observe	Dates:	
Set a date for post-programme assessments	Date:	
Complete evaluation and disseminate outcomes to SLT	Date:	

Intervention Plan

Name of provision	**FURTHER LITERACY SUPPORT (FLS)**
Aims of the programme	To generate accelerated learning back to the appropriate NLS Framework teaching objectives.
Description of programme	3 modules each lasting 4 weeks. Overall focus is on consolidating objectives from year 4 and year 5, terms 1 and 2. The main emphasis is on writing. Pupils use a workbook which is supplemented by optional homework. These sessions are additional to the daily literacy hour.
Target group	Year 5.
Entry level	3c.
Exit level	3a.
Length of intervention	12 weeks.
Frequency	30 mins per session.
Delivered by	TA, who has been trained to deliver the programme, delivers 3 sessions per week. Teacher delivers guided reading and guided writing.
Suggested start date	Spring term.
Groupings	Maximum 6.
Monitoring arrangements	Literacy coordinator to observe one session.
Assessment method	4 screenings.
	Book band level/running record.
	Writing sample.
	Flow chart – entry and exit.
	Progress checks.

Task	Date/Information	Checklist tick when completed
Identify children to be screened	Names:	
Set a date for screening	Date:	
Select children for the group	Names:	
Fix a timetable for the sessions each week	Times:	
Allocate half a day of preparation time for the TA	Date:	
Decide where the sessions will take place	Location:	
Fix a time for the weekly teacher/TA review session	Time:	
Set a date for the parent meeting	Date:	
Set a date for the intervention programme to begin	Date:	
Set a date for the progress checks during the programme	Date:	
Set a date for SENCO to observe session	Date:	
Set a date for post-programme assessments	Date:	
Complete evaluation and disseminate outcomes to SLT	Date:	

Intervention Plan

Name of provision	**SUPPORTING CHILDREN WITH GAPS IN THEIR MATHEMATICAL UNDERSTANDING (WAVE 3 MATHS)**
Aims of the programme	To increase children's rates of progress in mathematics by using targeted approaches to tackle fundamental errors and misconceptions.
Description of programme	The materials focus on number and calculation, tackling areas such as understanding the structure of number and operations between numbers. Problem-solving is integrated and exemplified in the materials, and opportunities are provided for children to develop mathematical vocabulary.
Target group	Aimed mainly at Key Stage 2 children who, for any reason, demonstrate fundamental errors and misconceptions that are preventing them making progress.
Entry level	Class teacher assessment that identifies significant errors and misconceptions.
Exit level	Class teacher assessment showing child no longer exhibits the error/misconception.
Length of intervention	Flexible.
Frequency	Flexible – short teaching sessions several times a week.
Delivered by	Ideally a teacher delivers the first teaching activity to tackle the error or misconception. This is then followed up with 'spotlight' sessions with a TA trained to deliver the programme.
Suggested start date	Flexible.
Groupings	1–1.
Assessment method	Tracking sheets, supplied in the pack.
	NC sub-level teacher assessment.
Monitoring arrangements	SENCO to observe TA once during the intervention.

Task	Date/Information	Checklist tick when completed
Select children to take part	Names:	
Class teacher assesses children using tracking charts	Date:	
Fix a timetable for the sessions each week	Times:	
Allocate half a day of preparation time for the TA	Date:	
Decide where the sessions will take place	Location:	
Fix a date when SENCO will monitor teaching	Date:	
Fix a time for the weekly teacher/ TA review session	Time:	
Set a date for the intervention programme to begin	Date:	
Set a date for the parent meeting	Date:	
Set a date for post-programme assessments	Date:	
Set dates for 3- and 6-month follow-up assessments	Date:	
Complete evaluation and disseminate outcomes to SLT	Date:	

Intervention Plan

Name of provision	SEAL FOCUS GROUP – MANAGING STRONG FEELINGS
Aims of the programme	To accelerate pupil progress towards SEAL learning outcomes. 'I understand why feelings sometimes "take over" or get out of control and know what makes me angry or upset', 'I have a range of strategies for managing impulses and strong emotions so they do not lead me to behave in ways that would have negative consequences for me or for other people.'
Description of programme	6, 2-hour small group sessions in school followed by 1 day off-site team challenge activities.
Target group	Year 8 pupils who have difficulty in managing strong feelings.
Entry level	Low scores on SEAL pupil and adult self-rating scale (managing feelings).
Exit level	
Length of intervention	7 weeks.
Frequency	Weekly.
Delivered by	LSU teacher and learning mentor (LM).
Suggested start date	Spring term.
Groupings	Maximum 8 with a balance of pupils – some impulsive, some easily upset, no more than 4 who are often angry.
Assessment method	Pupils who might benefit from the scheme are identified using self and tutor referral. Pupil, parent and form teacher rating scales are then used to select final group. The same rating scales are repeated at the end of the intervention. Evaluation is via changes to rating scales and reductions in number of times per month pupil is placed in detention or referred to HoY.

Task	Date/Information	Checklist tick when completed
Identify pupils who might benefit	Names:	
Set a date for pupil meetings (to secure sign-up and complete self-rating scales)	Date:	
Set a date for parent meetings (to include use of rating scales)	Date:	
Set a date for tutor completion of ratings scales	Date:	
Select pupils for the group	Names:	
Fix a timetable for the sessions each week	Times:	
Fix dates for initial planning (half day) and post-session reviews/forward planning for the teacher and LM	Dates:	
Decide where the sessions will take place	Location:	
Set a date for the intervention programme to begin	Date:	
Set a date for INCO to monitor	Date:	
Set a date for end of intervention post-programme assessments	Date:	
Set dates for 3- and 6-month follow-up assessments	Dates:	
Complete evaluation and disseminate outcomes to SLT	Date:	

Intervention Plan

Name of provision	**LEARNING CHALLENGE**
Aims of the programme	To help pupils improve their organisation of themselves and of their learning, so that they will be better equipped to take advantage of what is offered to them in lessons.
Description of programme	A series of 7 challenge activities covering a range of organisational skills.
Target group	KS3 pupils who are disorganised in their preparation for schoolwork or homework, or who have poorly developed learning strategies.
Entry level	Attainment in 1 or more of the core subjects that is up to 2 years below age-related expectations.
Exit level	
Length of intervention	Flexible.
Frequency	Flexible.
Delivered by	Volunteer coaches – TAs, parent volunteers, governors, form tutors, learning mentors, librarians, or other students.
Suggested start date	Flexible.
Groupings	1–1.
Assessment method	A target group of pupils who will benefit from the scheme is identified using the diagnostic tools provided in the materials.
	The teacher who is organising the scheme analyses the pupils' difficulties in organising their learning by means of an interview and information from subject teachers and form tutors, and sets pupil targets.
	The teacher organiser reassesses pupils at the end of the intervention against the targets set.
Monitoring arrangements	Organising teacher will observe all coaches at least once.

Task	Date/Information	Checklist tick when completed
Identify which pupils will be supported through the Learning Challenge	Names:	
Decide the extent and duration of support for each pupil		
Allocate pupils to coaches	Name: Coach:	
Fix a timetable for the sessions each week	Times:	
Decide where the sessions will take place	Location:	
Fix dates to monitor sessions	Dates:	
Fix times for support meetings coaches/ organising teacher	Time:	
Set a date for the intervention programme to begin	Date:	
Set a date for the parent meeting	Date:	
Set dates for observation of coaching	Dates:	
Set a date for post-programme assessments	Date:	
Complete evaluation and disseminate outcomes to SLT	Date:	

Record of Intervention Programme

WEEK COMMENCED												
Names	Pre-intervention assessment outcomes	Wk 1	Wk 2	Wk 3	Wk 4	Wk 5	Wk 6	Wk 7	Wk 8	Wk 9	Wk 10	Post-intervention assessment outcomes
Sessions run												
Weekly meeting with teacher												
Evaluation												

Notes:
Write in all dates in advance where possible.
Tick in the weekly box if the child attended the session.
Continue on further sheet where programmes last longer than 10 weeks.
If assessments are on another sheet, write 'see attached sheet' and staple to the record sheets.

Monitoring the Quality of Intervention Sessions

QUALITY FEATURES	✓	EVIDENCE
The right pupils have been targeted.		
The location is appropriate.		
The frequency of the intervention is as specified.		
The session length is as specified.		
The session content matches that specified in the programme.		
Resources have been pre-prepared and are well managed.		
The adult and the pupils know what the learning objectives are.		
The adult has sufficient subject knowledge to promote learning.		
The session is planned and adjusted on the basis of assessment and pupils are helped to identify their own learning targets and to assess their own progress.		
Key instructions and learning points are given concisely and clearly and repeated as necessary.		
Behaviour is well managed and the adult promotes interaction between the pupils in the group.		
The adult promotes pupils' independence as learners, helping them recognise what strategies they are using successfully and apply them in other situations.		
The adult creates a secure and supportive learning environment where there is safety to have a go and make mistakes.		
The adult challenges pupils and expects the most from them.		
Teaching styles and approaches are active, lively and multisensory; the session is well paced.		
Class or subject teacher and additional adult plan and review the intervention jointly.		
There are opportunities for pupils to apply their learning and have it reinforced in class/across the school.		
Parental involvement is secured as specified in the programme.		

Actions:

Intervention Data Collection

- Reading Recovery
- Fischer Family Trust Wave 3
- ELS
- ALS
- Y3LS
- FLS
- Rainbow Reading
- Other

SCHOOL: _____   YEAR _____

CHILDREN'S PROFILE				PRE-SCREENING DATE:						POST-SCREENING DATE:						OUTCOME	
NAME	DATE OF BIRTH	GENDER 1 = M 2 = F	YEAR GROUP	INTERVENTION	BOOK BAND LEVEL	NATIONAL CURRICULUM READING LEVEL	NATIONAL CURRICULUM WRITING LEVEL	PHONICS STAGE	READING AGE	BOOK BAND LEVEL	NATIONAL CURRICULUM READING LEVEL	NATIONAL CURRICULUM WRITING LEVEL	PHONICS STAGE	READING AGE	NUMBER OF LESSONS	ACTION 1 – MONITORING ONLY 2 – TOP UP SUPPORT 3 – WAVE 3 SUPPORT

Class Handover Profile

Class	Avg	Sept'07
	SA	RA

Class list	Reading – progress 06/07	Writing – progress 06/07	Maths – progress 06/07	Spell Age	Read Age	SEN STATUS				EAL	Looked after	Free school meals	Summer born	Poor attendance	Other issues e.g. bereavement
						SA+	ST'MT	SEN TYPE	G&T						

Legend:
- 2 sub-levels progress made
- 1 sub-level progress made
- 0 sub-levels progress made

References

Audit Commission (2002) *Special educational needs: a mainstream issue?* London: Audit Commission

Beard, R., Pell, G., Shorrocks-Taylor, D. and Swinnerton, B., with Sawyer, V., Willcocks, J. and Yeomans, D. (2005) *Follow-up study of the National Evaluation of the National Literacy Strategy Further Literacy Support Programme.* Reading: Centre for British Teachers

Black, P., Harrison, C., Lee, C., Marshall, B. and Wiliam, D. (2003) *Assessment for learning: putting it into practice.* Maidenhead: Open University Press

Blatchford, P., Martin, C., Moriarty, V., Bassett, P. and Goldstein, H. (2002) *Pupil: adult ratio differences and educational progress over Reception and Key Stage 1.* London: DfES

Blatchford, P., Russell, A., Bassett, P., Brown, P. and Martin, C. (2004) *The role and effects of teaching assistants in English primary schools (Years 4 to 6).* London: DfES

Brooks, G. (1996) *Family literacy works.* London: NFER/BSA

Brooks, G. (1998) *Family numeracy adds up.* London: NFER/BSA

Casey, J. (2007) *GCSEs: what can a parent do? 101 tips to ensure success.* Bristol: Futurelink Publishing

Centre for Studies in Inclusive Education (2002) *Index for inclusion.* Bristol: CSIE

Clarke, S. (2001) *Unlocking formative assessment.* London: Hodder and Stoughton

Cochrane, S. (2006) *Putting the pieces together: a guide to provision management.* London: London Regional Partnership

Cole, B. (2005) Mission impossible? Special educational needs, inclusion and the re-conceptualisation of the role of the SENCO in England and Wales. *European Journal of Special Needs Education,* 20 (3)

DCSF (2007a) *Social and emotional aspects of learning for secondary schools.* London: DCSF

DCSF (2007b) *Special Educational Needs in England: January 2007.* London: DCSF

Desforges, C. (2007) *Children in the secondary school age range with moderate special educational needs (MLD): a research review.* London: Esmée Fairbairn Foundation

Desforges, C. and Abouchaar, A. (2003) *The impact of parental involvement, parental support and family education on pupil achievement and adjustment: a review of the literature.* London: DfES

DfES (2001a) *SEN Toolkit.* London: DfES

DfES (2001b) *Special Educational Needs Code of Practice*. London: DfES

DfES (2003) *Models and images*. London: DfES

DfES (2004a) *Assessment for learning*. London: DfES

DfES (2004b) *Excellence and enjoyment: learning and teaching in the primary years*. London: DfES

DfES (2004c) *Learning and teaching for children with special educational needs in the primary years*. London: DfES

DfES (2004d) *Removing barriers to achievement: the government's strategy for SEN*. London: DfES

DfES (2004e) *Strengthening teaching and learning through the use of curricular targets*. London: DfES

DfES (2004f) *The intensifying support programme*. London: DfES

DfES (2005a) *Excellence and enjoyment: social and emotional aspects of learning*. London: DfES

DfES (2005b) *Higher standards, better schools for all*. London: DfES

DfES (2005c) *Leading on inclusion*. London: DfES

DfES (2005d) *Maximising progress: ensuring the attainment of pupils with SEN*. London: DfES

DfES (2005e) *Supporting children with gaps in their mathematical understanding*. London: DfES

DfES (2005f) *The effective management of teaching assistants to improve standards in literacy and mathematics*. London: DfES

DfES (2005g) *Tracking for success*. London: DfES

DfES (2006a) *Effective leadership: ensuring the progress of pupils with SEN and/or disabilities*. London: DfES

DfES (2006b) *Excellence and enjoyment: social and emotional aspects of learning: Family SEAL*. London: DfES

DfES (2006c) *Excellence and enjoyment: social and emotional aspects of learning: small group activities*. London: DfES

DfES (2006d) *Leading on intervention*. London: DfES

DfES (2006e) *Secondary intervention: progression maps*. London: DfES

DfES (2006f) *Strengthening teaching and learning through the use of curricular targets: the Intensifying Support Programme professional development meetings (PDMs)*. London: DfES

DfES (2006g) *2020 Vision. Report of the Teaching and Learning Review Group*. London: DfES

DfES (2007) *Making good progress*. London: DfES

Doyle, R. (2001) Using a readiness scale for reintegrating pupils with social, emotional and behavioural difficulties from a Nurture Group into their mainstream classroom – a pilot study. *British Journal of Special Education*, 28 (3)

Everard, B. and Morris, G. (1990) *Effective school management*. London: PCP

Feiler, A. (2003) A home visiting project for Reception children predicted to experience literacy difficulties. *British Journal of Special Education*, 30 (3)

Flouri, E. and Buchanan, A. (2002) What predicts good relationships with parents in adolescence and partners in adult life? *Journal of Family Psychology*, 16, 186–198

Freeman, J. (2001) *Gifted children grown up*. London: Taylor & Francis

Fullan, M. (2001) *The new meaning of educational change*, 3rd edn. Columbia: Teachers College Press

Gerber, S., Finn J., Achilles, C. and Boyd-Zaharias, J. (2001) Teacher aides and students' academic achievement. *Educational Evaluation and Policy Analysis*, 23 (2)

Giangreco, M., Cloninger, C. and Iverson, V. (1993) *Choosing options and accommodations for children (COACH): a guide to planning inclusive education*. Baltimore, MD: Paul H. Brookes

Giangreco, M., Edelman, S., Luisellu, T. and Macfarland, S. (1997) Helping or hovering? Effects of instructional assistant proximity on students with disabilities. *Exceptional Children*, 64, 7–18

Gross, J. (1994) Asperger Syndrome: a label worth having? *Educational Psychology in Practice*, 10 (2)

Gross, J. (1996) The weight of the evidence. *Support for Learning*, 11 (1)

Gross, J. (2000) Paper promises? Making the Code work for you. *Support for Learning*, 15 (3)

Gross, J. (2002) *Special educational needs in the primary school: a practical guide*, 3rd edn. Buckingham: Open University Press

Gross, J. and White, A. (2003) *Special educational needs and school improvement*. London: David Fulton

House of Commons Education and Skills Select Committee (2006) *Special educational needs: third report of session 2005–6*. London: HMSO

Howes, A. (2003) Teaching reforms and the impact of paid adult support on participation in learning in mainstream schools. *Support for Learning*, 18 (4)

Huberman, M. (1983) Recipes for busy kitchens: a situational analysis of routine knowledge use in schools. *Knowledge*, 4 (4)

Independent Review Unit (2006) *IRU Statement for 2006*. London: DfES

Independent Review Unit (2007) *IRU statement on SEN and disability: meeting need, minimising bureaucracy*. London: DfES

Jones, P. and Swain, J. (2001) Parents reviewing annual reviews. *British Journal of Special Education*, 28 (2)

Klein, R. (2000) *Defying disaffection*. London: Trentham Books

Knoster, T. (1991) Presentation at TASH conference, Washington DC (adapted by Knoster from Enterprise Group, Ltd)

KPMG Foundation (2006) *The long term costs of literacy difficulties*. London: KPMG Foundation

Lingard, T. (2001) Does the Code of Practice help secondary school SENCOs to improve learning? *British Journal of Special Education*, 28 (4)

Moyles, J. and Suschitzky, W. (1997) *Jills of all trades: classroom assistants in KS1 classes.* London: University of Leicester/ATL

National Institute for Health and Clinical Excellence (2006) *Parent-training education programmes in the management of children with conduct disorders.* NICE technology appraisal guidance, 102

Norwich, B. and Kelly, N. (2004) *A study of promising practices of pupil participation in SEN procedures in south-west mainstream schools.* Exeter: University of Exeter School of Lifelong Learning

NUT (2004) *Special educational needs co-ordinators and the revised Code of Practice: an NUT survey.* London: National Union of Teachers

Ofsted (1999) *The SEN Code of Practice: three years on.* London: Ofsted

Ofsted (2004) *Special educational needs and disability: towards inclusive schools.* London: Ofsted

Ofsted (2006a) *Inclusion: does it matter where pupils are taught?* London: Ofsted

Ofsted (2006b) *The Annual Report of Her Majesty's Chief Inspector of Schools.* London: Ofsted

Papps, I. and Dyson, A. (2004) *The costs and benefits of earlier identification and effective intervention.* London: DfES

Pinkus, S. (2005) Bridging the gap between policy and practice: adopting a strategic vision for partnership working in special education. *British Journal of Special Education*, 32 (4)

Pinney, A. (2004) *Reducing reliance on statements: an investigation into local authority practice and outcomes.* London: DfES

QCA (2000) The National Curriculum for England. London: QCA

Rathbone (2001) An analysis of how well mainstream schools involve the parents of pupils with SEN. *Special Education Advice*, Spring 2001. Manchester: Rathbone

Scott, S., Spender, Q., Doolan, M., Jacobs, B. and Aspland, H. (2001) Multicentre controlled trial of parenting groups for childhood antisocial behaviour in clinical practice. *British Medical Journal*, 323, 1–7

Sylva, K., Melhuish, E., Sammons, P., Siraj-Blatchford, I., Taggart, B. and Elliot, K. (2003) *The effective provision of pre-school education (EPPE) project: findings from the pre-school period.* London: Institute of Education, University of London

Tymms, P. and Merrell, C. (2006) Screening and interventions for inattentive, hyperactive and impulsive children. *European Journal of Special Needs Education*, 21 (3)

Wedell, K. (2002) What is additional and different about IEPs? *British Journal of Special Education*, 29 (4)

Index

Figures are indicated by **bold** page numbers, tables by *italics*.